The Sarbanes–Oxley Act

Overview and Implementation Procedures Manual

Michael F. Holt

AMSTERDAM • BOSTON • HEIDELBERG • LONDON
NEW YORK • OXFORD • PARIS • SAN DIEGO
SAN FRANCISCO • SINGAPORE • SYDNEY • TOKYO

CIMA Publishing is an imprint of Elsevier

CIMA Publishing
An imprint of Elsevier
Linacre House, Jordan Hill, Oxford OX2 8DP
30 Corporate Drive, Burlington, MA 01803

First published 2006

British Library Cataloguing in Publication Data
A catalogue record for this book is available from the British Library

Library of Congress Cataloguing in Publication Data
A catalogue record for this book is available from the Library of Congress

ISBN   0 7506 6823 7
ISBN   978 0 7506 6823 1

For information on all CIMA Publishing Publications
visit our website at www.cimapublishing.com

Typeset by Integra Software Services Pvt. Ltd, Pondicherry, India
www.integra-india.com
Printed and bound in Great Britain

Working together to grow
libraries in developing countries

www.elsevier.com | www.bookaid.org | www.sabre.org

ELSEVIER   BOOK AID
             International   Sabre Foundation

Acknowledgements

The Government of the United States
and the Securities Exchange Commission

for

The Sarbanes–Oxley Act of 2002
The Final Rules
SE Act 10A

The American Institute of Certified Public Accountants

for

The COSO Framework

The various companies offering commercial SOX Solutions
(descriptions taken verbatim from their respective websites)

Mr. Mark Perry of
BOT International Inc.

and

Mr. Mike Barry of
VCom Inc.

Disclaimer

This book is intended as a guide only and contains no guarantee that following the guidelines contained herein will ensure full compliance with the requirements of the Sarbanes–Oxley Act.

Readers are responsible for ensuring their own compliance with the Sarbanes–Oxley Act. It is the reader's sole responsibility to obtain advice of competent legal counsel as to the identification and interpretation of any relevant laws, including but not limited to, the Sarbanes–Oxley Act, that may affect the reader's business and any actions the reader may need to take to comply with such laws. Michael F. Holt and/or the Publishers do not provide legal, audit or accounting advice or represent or warrant that following the contents of this book, or using the templates provided in the book or on the accompanying CD, will ensure that a company is in compliance with any law.

The Author, Michael F. Holt, welcomes comment and analysis regarding this book and the Sarbanes–Oxley Act and can be contacted as follows:

Box 8486, Victoria, British Columbia, Canada V8W3S1

Tel: (250) 889-0511 • e-mail: **mike@logiclynx.com**

Contents

Background

The Sarbanes–Oxley Act was passed at the One Hundred and Seventh Congress of the United States of America in January, 2002. It purports to be an act to "Protect investors by improving the accuracy and reliability of corporate disclosures made pursuant to the securities laws, and for other purposes".

While this is an American Act, it applies to every corporation listed on a United States Stock Exchange, or to *ANY non-US corporation that meets the criteria as a Foreign Private Issuer,* or to any entity which solicits funds for investment in the USA (see Chapter 1 "Definitions"). Further, other countries including the UK and Canada are introducing similar legislation to govern corporations operating domestically. In general, Europe seems to favour a "principles" based system as opposed the US "rules" based approach.

It is, therefore, appropriate and probably necessary for most corporations to comply with Sarbanes–Oxley requirements in order to avoid future problems with the governing bodies. Non-public companies contemplating an IPO or anticipating an acquisition/merger situation can also benefit from implementing the system since it will make them a much more attractive proposition and greatly reduce compliance difficulties later.

While the costs of implementing an Internal Control System to meet the SOX requirements can be considerable, it isn't by any means money wasted. The improved efficiencies and information gathering will benefit most companies by providing useful risk management, employee accountability, performance management and communications at the very least.

This book summarizes the Act and provides a simplified guide to compliance. The purpose is to provide management with a reasonably accurate idea of what Sarbanes–Oxley compliance entails. Detailed procedural manuals and dedicated software packages for satisfying the requirements of sections 302 and 404 are available from a variety of sources.

Auditor's responsibilities and compliance are not included in this manual in detail.

Full-sized, usable templates are provided in the accompanying CD with this book, along with a PowerPoint presentation which explains to employees and Board members the background and need for an Internal Control system.

It is apparent that it will be a full-time job for at least one individual and probably several to establish and maintain a system for compliance, and to keep up with the changes and amendments that are a feature of this legislation. Since the main thrust of the requirements are for financial accountability and control, it will likely fall on the accounting personnel to perform these functions. However, the Internal Control System appears to also be required (Section 302) to address any material information that will affect the financial well-being of the company.

Senior management should be aware of the scope and implications of the Act and the need for compliance as well as having an understanding of what the company is doing to ensure compliance.

References and Other Useful Materials

For the full text of the Sarbanes–Oxley Act, go to:

http://www.thecre.com/fedlaw/topicals.htm

And click on:

Sarbanes–Oxley Act of 2002 (aka Corporate and Auditing Accountability, Responsibility, and Transparency Act of 2002)

or at

http://www.law.uc.edu/CCL/SOact/toc.html

SEC Final Rules complete text is at:

http://www.sec.gov/rules/final/33-8238.htm

Some useful summaries can be found at:

http://www.valuebasedmanagement.net/organizations_sarbanes.html
http://www.aicpa.org/info/sarbanes_oxley_summary.htm
http://www.accountancyage.com/News/1131123

A useful "White Paper Proposing Practical, Cost Effective Compliance Strategies" is found at:

http://www.sec.gov/rules/proposed/s74002/card941503.pdf

The up-to-date Internal Controls Framework document prepared by COSO can be obtained from the American Institute of Certified Public Accountants at www.aicpa.org

An on-going website describing changes, questions and answers, news and current events concerning SOX is available at http://sarbanes-oxley.com.

Quotes from ACL

ACL Services Ltd. is a global provider of Business Assurance solutions to financial executives and audit professionals.

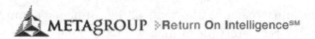

Stocking the Compliance Toolbox to Meet SOX Section 404

John Van Decker, Stan Lepeak – The official date for compliance with Sarbanes–Oxley Act (SOX) Section 404, requiring publicly traded US companies to document/certify financial processes, has been extended for companies whose FY04 close is June 15, 2004, or later. This gives most companies extra time to address compliance by leveraging new enterprise risk-management consulting/business applications and offerings from both enterprise (e.g. independent software vendors) and business/IT service providers.

Various compliance point solutions (e.g. from Plumtree, OpenPages, ACL, Steelpoint, and CXO Systems) include tools to manage risk programs, document enterprise business processes, capture/store regulated communications, and track key risk-management indicators. Although some of these solutions will play a longer-term role (e.g. enterprise portals), compliance will ultimately be supported through applications such as enterprise content management (ECM) and enterprise resource planning (ERP; e.g. Documentum and Oracle have announced SOX offerings). However, it will take 1–3 years for enterprise ISVs to penetrate this market. Companies should selectively invest in point solutions to meet near-term regulatory deadlines but recognize that long-term compliance is a comprehensive enterprise-wide effort.

Tax/audit firms (e.g. Deloitte, PwC, KPMG, E&Y) and related compliance vendors (e.g. Protiviti, Jefferson Wells) have SOX service offerings and some supporting software tools. However, these firms' long-term play (except for hybrid Deloitte) will be related to process analysis and risk assessment, not software/IT services. The larger service play (2–3 + years out) will come from more traditional

IT service providers (e.g. BearingPoint, IBM) deploying/customizing enterprise applications.

Bottom Line

Organizations must balance the tactical investments required to meet short-term regulatory deadlines with the long-term requirements to strategically manage overall regulatory demands while simultaneously improving business performance and efficiency. Compliance-related projects may dwarf previous Y2K efforts (META/FACTS, 10 June 2003).

xii

SOX Section 404: Best to Start With a "Data Audit"

John Van Decker – *Application Delivery Strategies, Enterprise Analytics Strategies*

Many North American public firms are scrutinizing major financial business processes as part of an enterprise risk-management initiative. Under Sarbanes–Oxley (SOX) Act Section 404, firms must perform a self-assessment of risk (with auditor attestation) for business processes that affect financial reporting. Unfortunately, the current enterprise-wide approach typical in many organizations includes documentation/review of all processes, and we suspect that this goes beyond the scope of what will be eventually required. Because materiality will be a prime consideration, firms should focus and implement data audit/analysis tools centered on business process auditing (e.g. ACL, TeamMate) to first identify fraud/process breakage when developing an enterprise risk-management program.

Bottom Line

Given heightened requirements for SOX compliance, the use of data auditing tools positioned for both internal and external auditors has been resurrected and should be considered. *(META Group Client Advisor 2018, 27 May 2003)*

Introduction

In this book, we will look at each section of the Sarbanes–Oxley Act and determine what actions are required by the typical small- to medium-sized corporations wishing to comply. It will be apparent that Sections 302, 404 (and 906) represent the tip of the iceberg and the aspect of the Act that is causing the greatest expense and difficulty. There is considerable room for interpretation of Section 302, in that the internal control system, while directly aimed at financial controls, also implies that other "material information" must be controlled in the same manner. In other words, anything that may affect the financial well-being of the company must be dealt with by the internal control system.

While the entire Act is relevant, some parts apply to Auditors and are not considered herein, while others do not require any action on the part of the Corporation for compliance. It is advisable of course that the Financial Officers of the corporation become familiar with the entire contents of the Act.

The preamble of the Sarbanes–Oxley Act is provided hereunder for reference. Following that is a summary of the Act itself with my comments regarding actions to be taken. By a summary, I mean that I have only presented the full text of a section of the act where it is required for understanding. For example, Section 101 describes in detail how the Board was established and how it is to perform its duties. None of this is required for our purposes here, so I simply summarized it as "Administrative Details for the Board". Obviously it would be advantageous for those persons in a Company who are taking on the job of setting up the compliance and internal controls system to read the Act in its entirety.

The Sarbanes–Oxley Act

One Hundred Seventh Congress
of the
United States of America

AT THE SECOND SESSION

Begun and held at the City of Washington on Wednesday,
the twenty-third day of January, two thousand and two

An Act

To protect investors by improving the accuracy and reliability of corporate disclosures
made pursuant to the securities laws, and for other purposes.

Be it enacted by the Senate and House of Representatives of
the United States of America in Congress assembled

SECTION 1. SHORT TITLE; TABLE OF CONTENTS

(a) SHORT TITLE—This Act may be cited as the "Sarbanes–Oxley Act of 2002"

(b) TABLE OF CONTENTS—The table of contents for this Act is as follows:

TITLE III—CORPORATE RESPONSIBILITY

TITLE IV—ENHANCED FINANCIAL DISCLOSURES

TITLE V—ANALYST CONFLICTS OF INTEREST

TITLE VI—COMMISSION RESOURCES AND AUTHORITY

TITLE VII—STUDIES AND REPORTS

TITLE VIII—CORPORATE AND CRIMINAL FRAUD ACCOUNTABILITY

TITLE IX—WHITE-COLLAR CRIME PENALTY ENHANCEMENTS

TITLE X—CORPORATE TAX RETURNS

TITLE XI—CORPORATE FRAUD AND ACCOUNTABILITY

SEC. 2. DEFINITIONS

(a) IN GENERAL—In this Act, the following definitions shall apply:

(1) APPROPRIATE STATE REGULATORY AUTHORITY—The term "appropriate State regulatory authority" means the State agency or other authority responsible for the licensure or other regulation of the practice of accounting in the State or States having jurisdiction over a registered public accounting firm or associated person thereof, with respect to the matter in question.

(2) AUDIT—The term "audit" means an examination of the financial statements of any issuer by an independent public accounting firm in accordance with the rules of the Board or the Commission (or, for the period preceding the adoption of applicable rules of the Board under section 103, in accordance with then-applicable generally accepted auditing and related standards for such purposes), for the purpose of expressing an opinion on such statements.

(3) AUDIT COMMITTEE—The term "audit committee" means—

(A) a committee (or equivalent body) established by and amongst the board of directors of an issuer for the purpose of overseeing the accounting and financial reporting processes of the issuer and audits of the financial statements of the issuer; and

    (B) if no such committee exists with respect to an issuer, the entire board of directors of the issuer.

(4) AUDIT REPORT—The term "audit report" means a document or other record—

    (A) prepared following an audit performed for purposes of compliance by an issuer with the requirements of the securities laws; and

    (B) in which a public accounting firm either—

        (i) sets forth the opinion of that firm regarding a financial statement, report, or other document; or

        (ii) asserts that no such opinion can be expressed.

(5) BOARD—The term "Board" means the Public Company Accounting Oversight Board established under section 101.

(6) COMMISSION—The term "Commission" means the Securities and Exchange Commission.

(7) ISSUER—The term "issuer" means an issuer (as defined in section 3 of the Securities Exchange Act of 1934 (15 U.S.C. 78c)), the securities of which are registered under section 12 of that Act (15 U.S.C. 78l), or that is required to file reports under section 15(d) (15 U.S.C. 78o(d)), or that files or has filed a registration statement that has not yet become effective under the Securities Act of 1933 (15 U.S.C. 77a et seq.), and that it has not withdrawn.

Note: Following is the extract from Section 3 of the 1934 Act related to "Issuers."

The term "issuer" means any person who issues or proposes to issue any security; except that with respect to certificates of deposit for securities, voting-trust certificates, or collateral-trust certificates, or with respect to certificates of interest or shares in an unincorporated investment trust not having a board of directors or of the fixed, restricted management, or unit type, the term "issuer" means the person or persons performing the acts and assuming the duties of depositor or manager pursuant to the provisions of the trust or other agreement or instrument under which such securities are issued; and except that with respect to equipment-trust certificates or like securities, the term "issuer" means the person by whom the equipment or property is, or is to be, used.

The term "person" means a natural person, company, government, or political subdivision, agency, or instrumentality of a government.

The term "security" means any note, stock, treasury stock, security future, bond, debenture, certificate of interest or participation in any profit-sharing agreement or in any oil, gas, or other mineral royalty or lease, any collateral-trust certificate, pre-organization certificate or subscription, transferable share, investment contract, voting-trust certificate, certificate of deposit for a security, any put, call, straddle, option, or privilege on any security, certificate of deposit, or group or index of securities (including any interest therein or based on the value thereof), or any put, call, straddle, option, or privilege entered into on a national securities exchange relating to foreign currency, or in general, any instrument commonly known as a "security"; or any certificate of interest or participation in, temporary or interim certificate for, receipt for, or warrant or right to subscribe to or purchase, any of the foregoing; but shall not include currency or any note, draft, bill of exchange, or banker's acceptance which has a maturity at the time of issuance of not exceeding nine months, exclusive of days of grace, or any renewal thereof the maturity of which is likewise limited.

Also, for non-US companies, this rule applies

Foreign private issuer

The term foreign private issuer means any foreign issuer other than a foreign government except an issuer meeting the following conditions:

(A) More than 50 percent of the outstanding voting securities of such issuer are directly or indirectly owned of record by residents of the United States; and any of the following:

(B) The majority of the executive officers or directors are United States citizens or residents;

(C) More than 50 percent of the assets of the issuer are located in the United States; or

(D) The business of the issuer is administered principally in the United States.

(8) NON-AUDIT SERVICES—The term "non-audit services" means any professional services provided to an issuer by a registered public accounting firm, other than those provided to an issuer in connection with an audit or a review of the financial statements of an issuer.

(9) PERSON ASSOCIATED WITH A PUBLIC ACCOUNTING FIRM—

(A) IN GENERAL—The terms "person associated with a public accounting firm" (or with a "registered public accounting firm") and "associated person of a public accounting firm" (or of a "registered public accounting firm") mean any individual proprietor, partner, shareholder, principal, accountant, or other professional employee of a public accounting firm, or any other independent contractor or entity that, in connection with the preparation or issuance of any audit report—

(i) shares in the profits of, or receives compensation in any other form from, that firm; or

(ii) participates as agent or otherwise on behalf of such accounting firm in any activity of that firm.

(B) EXEMPTION AUTHORITY—The Board may, by rule, exempt persons engaged only in ministerial tasks from the definition in subparagraph (A), to the extent that the Board determines that any such exemption is consistent with the purposes of this Act, the public interest, or the protection of investors.

(10) PROFESSIONAL STANDARDS—The term "professional standards" means—

(A) accounting principles that are—

(i) established by the standard setting body described in section 19(b) of the Securities Act of 1933, as amended by this Act, or prescribed by the Commission under section 19(a) of that Act (15 U.S.C. 17a(s)) or section 13(b) of the Securities Exchange Act of 1934 (15 U.S.C. 78a(m)); and

(ii) relevant to audit reports for particular issuers, or dealt with in the quality control system of a particular registered public accounting firm; and

(B) auditing standards, standards for attestation engagements, quality control policies and procedures, ethical and competency standards, and independence standards (including rules implementing title II) that the Board or the Commission determines—

(i) relate to the preparation or issuance of audit reports for issuers; and

(ii) are established or adopted by the Board under section 103(a), or are promulgated as rules of the Commission.

(11) PUBLIC ACCOUNTING FIRM—The term "public accounting firm" means—

(A) a proprietorship, partnership, incorporated association, corporation, limited liability company, limited liability partnership, or other legal entity that is engaged in the practice of public accounting or preparing or issuing audit reports; and

(B) to the extent so designated by the rules of the Board, any associated person of any entity described in subparagraph (A).

(12) REGISTERED PUBLIC ACCOUNTING FIRM—The term "registered public accounting firm" means a public accounting firm registered with the Board in accordance with this Act.

(13) RULES OF THE BOARD—The term "rules of the Board" means the bylaws and rules of the Board (as submitted to, and approved, modified, or amended by the Commission, in accordance with section 107), and those stated policies, practices, and interpretations of the Board that the Commission, by rule, may deem to be rules of the Board, as necessary or appropriate in the public interest or for the protection of investors.

(14) SECURITY—The term "security" has the same meaning as in section 3(a) of the Securities Exchange Act of 1934 (15 U.S.C. 78c(a)).

(15) SECURITIES LAWS—The term "securities laws" means the provisions of law referred to in section 3(a)(47) of the Securities Exchange Act of 1934 (15 U.S.C. 78c(a)(47)), as amended by this Act, and includes the rules, regulations, and orders issued by the Commission thereunder.

(16) STATE—The term "State" means any State of the United States, the District of Columbia, Puerto Rico, the Virgin Islands, or any other territory or possession of the United States.

(b) CONFORMING AMENDMENT—Section 3(a)(47) of the Securities Exchange Act of 1934 (15 U.S.C. 78c(a)(47)) is amended by inserting "the Sarbanes–Oxley Act of 2002," before "the Public."

SEC. 3. COMMISSION RULES AND ENFORCEMENT

(a) REGULATORY ACTION—The Commission shall promulgate such rules and regulations, as may be necessary or appropriate in the public interest or for the protection of investors, and in further-ance of this Act.

(b) ENFORCEMENT—

(1) IN GENERAL—A violation by any person of this Act, any rule or regulation of the Commission issued under this Act, or any rule of the Board shall be treated for all purposes in the same manner as a violation of the Securities Exchange Act of 1934 (15 U.S.C. 78a et seq.) or the rules and regulations issued thereunder, consistent with the provisions of this Act, and any such person shall be subject to the same penal-ties, and to the same extent, as for a violation of that Act or such rules or regulations.

(2) INVESTIGATIONS, INJUNCTIONS, AND PROSECUTION OF OFFENSES—Section 21 of the Securities Exchange Act of 1934 (15 U.S.C. 78u) is amended—
   (A) in subsection (a)(1), by inserting "the rules of the Public Company Accounting Oversight Board, of which such person is a registered public accounting firm or a person associated with such a firm," after "is a participant,"
   (B) in subsection (d)(1), by inserting "the rules of the Public Company Accounting Oversight Board, of which such

person is a registered public accounting firm or a person associated with such a firm," after "is a participant,";

 (C) in subsection (e), by inserting "the rules of the Public Company Accounting Oversight Board, of which such person is a registered public accounting firm or a person associated with such a firm," after "is a participant,"; and

 (D) in subsection (f), by inserting "or the Public Company Accounting Oversight Board" after "self-regulatory organization" each place that term appears.

(3) CEASE-AND-DESIST PROCEEDINGS—Section 21C(c)(2) of the Securities Exchange Act of 1934 (15 U.S.C. 78u-3(c)(2)) is amended by inserting "registered public accounting firm (as defined in section 2 of the Sarbanes–Oxley Act of 2002)," after "government securities dealer,".

(4) ENFORCEMENT BY FEDERAL BANKING AGENCIES— Section 12(i) of the Securities Exchange Act of 1934 (15 U.S.C. 78l(i)) is amended by—

 (A) striking "sections 12," each place it appears and inserting "sections 10A(m), 12,"; and (B) striking "and 16," each place it appears and inserting "and 16 of this Act, and sections 302, 303, 304, 306, 401(b), 404, 406, and 407 of the Sarbanes–Oxley Act of 2002,".

(c) EFFECT ON COMMISSION AUTHORITY—Nothing in this Act or the rules of the Board shall be construed to impair or limit—

(1) the authority of the Commission to regulate the accounting profession, accounting firms, or persons associated with such firms for purposes of enforcement of the securities laws;

(2) the authority of the Commission to set standards for accounting or auditing practices or auditor independence, derived from other provisions of the securities laws or the rules or regulations thereunder, for purposes of the preparation and issuance of any audit report, or otherwise under applicable law; or

(3) the ability of the Commission to take, on the initiative of the Commission, legal, administrative, or disciplinary action against any registered public accounting firm or any associated person thereof.

Title I—Public company accounting oversight board

Sec. 101. Establishment; administrative provisions

Summary

This section provides administrative details for the Board. (Public Company Accounting Oversight Board)

Action Required

None

Sec. 102. Registration with the Board

Summary

MANDATORY REGISTRATION—Beginning 180 days after the date of the determination of the Commission under section 101(d), it shall be unlawful for any person that is not a registered public accounting firm to prepare or issue, or to participate in the preparation or issuance of, any audit report with respect to any issuer.

Action Required

Obtain written confirmation that the company's auditors are registered. (Template 1.1)

Sec. 103. Auditing, quality control, and independence standards and rules

Summary

AUDITING, QUALITY CONTROL, AND ETHICS STANDARDS—
(1) IN GENERAL—The Board shall, by rule, establish, including, to the extent it determines appropriate, through adoption of standards proposed by 1 or more professional groups of accountants designated pursuant to paragraph (3)(A) or advisory groups convened pursuant to paragraph (4), and amend or otherwise modify or alter, such auditing and related

attestation standards, such quality control standards, and such ethics standards to be used by registered public accounting firms in the preparation and issuance of audit reports, as required by this Act or the rules of the Commission, or as may be necessary or appropriate in the public interest or for the protection of investors.

Action Required

Obtain written confirmation that the Company's auditors comply with the quality control and ethics rules of the Board. (Template 1.2)

Sec. 104. Inspections of registered public accounting firms

Summary

IN GENERAL—The Board shall conduct a continuing program of inspections to assess the degree of compliance of each registered public accounting firm and associated persons of that firm with this Act, the rules of the Board, the rules of the Commission, or professional standards, in connection with its performance of audits, issuance of audit reports, and related matters involving issuers.

Action Required

None

Sec. 105. Investigations and disciplinary proceedings

Summary

IN GENERAL—The Board shall establish, by rule, subject to the requirements of this section, fair procedures for the investigation and disciplining of registered public accounting firms and associated persons of such firms.

Action Required

None, but it might be advisable to ask the company's auditors if they have ever been investigated by the Board and if so, what was the outcome.

Sec. 106. Foreign public accounting firms

Summary

APPLICABILITY TO CERTAIN FOREIGN FIRMS—
IN GENERAL—Any foreign public accounting firm
that prepares or furnishes an audit report with
respect to any issuer, shall be subject to this Act and
the rules of the Board and the Commission issued
under this Act, in the same manner and to the same
extent as a public accounting firm that is organized
and operates under the laws of the United States
or any State, except that registration pursuant to
section 102 shall not by itself provide a basis for
subjecting such a foreign public accounting firm to
the jurisdiction of the Federal or State courts, other
than with respect to controversies between such
firms and the Board.

Action Required

If the Company has a non-US accounting firm and is listed in the
US, ensure by written confirmation that the auditing firm does and
will conform to the requirements of the Act. (Template 1.3)

Sec. 107. Commission oversight of the Board

Summary

GENERAL OVERSIGHT RESPONSIBILITY—The
Commission shall have oversight and enforcement
authority over the Board, as provided in this Act.
The provisions of section 17(a)(1) of the Securities
Exchange Act of 1934 (15 U.S.C. 78q(a)(1)), and
of section 17(b)(1) of the Securities Exchange Act of
1934 (15 U.S.C. 78q(b)(1)) shall apply to the Board
as fully as if the Board were a "registered securities
association" for purposes of those sections 17(a)(1)
and 17(b)(1).

Action Required

None (Commission is the SEC)

Sec. 108. Accounting standards

Summary

IN GENERAL—In carrying out its authority under subsection (a) and under section 13(b) of the Securities Exchange Act of 1934, the Commission may recognize, as "generally accepted" for purposes of the securities laws, any accounting principles established by a standard setting body . . .

Action Required

Ensure that the accounting system used by the company is "generally accepted". The company's auditors can be requested to provide written confirmation that the system is acceptable. (Template 1.4)

Sec. 109. Funding

Summary

IN GENERAL—The Board, and the standard setting body designated pursuant to section 19(b) of the Securities Act of 1933, as amended by section 108, shall be funded as provided in this section.

Action Required

None

Title II—Auditor independence

Sec. 201. Services outside the scope of practice of auditors

Summary

PROHIBITED ACTIVITIES—Except as provided in subsection (h), it shall be unlawful for a registered public accounting firm (and any associated person of that firm, to the extent determined appropriate by the Commission) that performs for any issuer any audit required by this title or the rules of the Commission under this title or, beginning 180 days after the date of commencement of the operations of the Public Company Accounting Oversight Board established under section 101 of the Sarbanes–Oxley Act of 2002 (in this section referred to as the "Board"), the rules of the Board, to provide to that issuer, contemporaneously with the audit, any non-audit service, including—

(1) bookkeeping or other services related to the accounting records or financial statements of the audit client;
(2) financial information systems design and implementation;
(3) appraisal or valuation services, fairness opinions, or contribution-in-kind reports;
(4) actuarial services;
(5) internal audit outsourcing services;
(6) management functions or human resources;
(7) broker or dealer, investment adviser, or investment banking services;
(8) legal services and expert services unrelated to the audit; and
(9) any other service that the Board determines, by regulation, is impermissible.

(h) PREAPPROVAL REQUIRED FOR NON-AUDIT SERVICES—A registered public accounting firm may engage in any non-audit service, including tax services, that is not described in any of paragraphs (1) through (9) of subsection (g) for an audit client, only if the activity is approved in advance by the audit committee of the issuer, in accordance with subsection (i).

EXEMPTION AUTHORITY—The Board may, on a case by case basis, exempt any person, issuer, public accounting firm, or transaction from the prohibition on the provision of services under section 10A(g) of the Securities Exchange Act of 1934 (as added by this section), to the extent that such exemption is necessary or appropriate in the public interest and is consistent with the protection of investors, and subject to review by the Commission in the same manner as for rules of the Board under section 107.

Action Required

Ensure that any and all of the listed services are being provided by other than the auditors or any firm connected to the auditors. (Template 2.1) Include the prohibitions in the company's Policies and Procedures Manual.

Sec. 202. Pre-approval requirements

Summary

AUDIT COMMITTEE ACTION—All auditing services (which may entail providing comfort letters in connection with securities underwritings or statutory audits required for insurance companies for purposes of State law) and non-audit services other than as provided in subparagraph (B), provided to an issuer by the auditor of the issuer shall be pre-approved by the audit committee of the issuer.

Action Required

Ensure that the audit committee is fully aware of the requirements of sections 201 and 202 in detail if such pre-approval of services is to be obtained.

Sec. 203. Audit partner rotation

Summary

> AUDIT PARTNER ROTATION—It shall be unlawful for a registered public accounting firm to provide audit services to an issuer if the lead (or coordinating) audit partner (having primary responsibility for the audit), or the audit partner responsible for reviewing the audit, has performed audit services for that issuer in each of the 5 previous fiscal years of that issuer.

Action Required

Retain records on an annual basis of the participants in the audits for the Company and check that this requirement is observed. (Template 2.2)

Sec. 204. Auditor reports to audit committees

Summary

> REPORTS TO AUDIT COMMITTEES—Each registered public accounting firm that performs for any issuer any audit required by this title shall timely report to the audit committee of the issuer—
>
> (1) all critical accounting policies and practices to be used;
>
> (2) all alternative treatments of financial information within generally accepted accounting principles that have been discussed with management officials of the issuer, ramifications of the use of such alternative disclosures and treatments, and the treatment preferred by the registered public accounting firm; and
>
> (3) other material written communications between the registered public accounting firm and the management of the issuer, such as any management letter or schedule of unadjusted differences.

Action Required

Ensure all of the discussions and reports are in writing and are retained by the company. (Template 2.3 – binder cover page)

Sec. 205. Conforming amendments

Summary

AUDIT COMMITTEE—The term "audit committee" means—

(A) a committee (or equivalent body) established by and amongst the board of directors of an issuer for the purpose of overseeing the accounting and financial reporting processes of the issuer and audits of the financial statements of the issuer; and

(B) if no such committee exists with respect to an issuer, the entire board of directors of the issuer.

Action Required

Establish an Audit Committee if one does not exist. (Template 2.4) Note that in this section, the term "Independent Public Accountant" has been replaced throughout with "Registered Public Accountant." This means that the accounting firm conducting any audit functions must be registered with the Board.

Sec. 206. Conflicts of interest

Summary

CONFLICTS OF INTEREST—It shall be unlawful for a registered public accounting firm to perform for an issuer any audit service required by this title, if a chief executive officer, controller, chief financial officer, chief accounting officer, or any person serving in an equivalent position for the issuer, was employed by that registered independent public accounting firm and participated in any capacity in the audit of that issuer during the 1-year period preceding the date of the initiation of the audit.

Action Required

None, unless the conflict exists, in which case it is remedied by changing auditors or re-assigning officers.

Sec. 207. Study of mandatory rotation of registered public accounting firms

Summary

STUDY AND REVIEW REQUIRED—The Comptroller General of the United States shall conduct a study and review of the potential effects of requiring the mandatory rotation of registered public accounting firms.

Action Required

None at this time. (Check to find out results of review)

Sec. 208. Commission authority

Summary

COMMISSION REGULATIONS—Not later than 180 days after the date of enactment of this Act, the Commission shall issue final regulations to carry out each of subsections (g) through (l) of section 10A of the Securities Exchange Act of 1934, as added by this title.

(b) AUDITOR INDEPENDENCE—It shall be unlawful for any registered public accounting firm (or an associated person thereof, as applicable) to prepare or issue any audit report with respect to any issuer, if the firm or associated person engages in any activity with respect to that issuer prohibited by any of subsections (g) through (l) of section 10A of the Securities Exchange Act of 1934, as added by this title, or any rule or regulation of the Commission or of the Board issued thereunder.

Action Required

Check section 10A (Appendix B), see Appendix A—Final Rules

Sec. 209. Considerations by appropriate State regulatory authorities

Summary

In supervising non-registered public accounting firms and their associated persons, appropriate State regulatory authorities should make an independent determination of the proper standards applicable, particularly taking into consideration the size and nature of the business of the accounting firms they supervise and the size and nature of the business of the clients of those firms. The standards applied by the Board under this Act should not be presumed to be applicable for purposes of this section for small- and medium-sized non-registered public accounting firms.

Action Required

None

Title III—Corporate responsibility

Sec. 301. Public company audit committees

Summary

(1) COMMISSION RULES

    (A) IN GENERAL—Effective not later than 270 days after the date of enactment of this subsection, the Commission shall, by rule, direct the national securities exchanges and national securities associations to prohibit the listing of any security of an issuer that is not in compliance with the requirements of any portion of paragraphs (2) through (6). (Section 10A SEC)

    (B) OPPORTUNITY TO CURE DEFECTS—The rules of the Commission under subparagraph (A) shall provide for appropriate procedures for an issuer to have an opportunity to cure any defects that would be the basis for a prohibition under subparagraph (A), before the imposition of such prohibition.

(2) RESPONSIBILITIES RELATING TO REGISTERED PUBLIC ACCOUNTING FIRMS—The audit committee of each issuer, in its capacity as a committee of the board of directors, shall be directly responsible for the appointment, compensation, and oversight of the work of any registered public accounting firm employed by that issuer (including resolution of disagreements between management and the auditor regarding financial reporting) for the purpose of preparing or issuing an audit report or related work, and each such registered public accounting firm shall report directly to the audit committee.

(3) INDEPENDENCE—

    (A) IN GENERAL—Each member of the audit committee of the issuer shall be a member of the board of directors of the issuer, and shall otherwise be independent.

(B) CRITERIA—In order to be considered to be independent for purposes of this paragraph, a member of an audit committee of an issuer may not, other than in his or her capacity as a member of the audit committee, the board of directors, or any other board committee—

accept any consulting, advisory, or other compensatory fee from the issuer; or

(ii) be an affiliated person of the issuer or any subsidiary thereof.

(C) EXEMPTION AUTHORITY—The Commission may exempt from the requirements of subparagraph (B) a particular relationship with respect to audit committee members, as the Commission determines appropriate in light of the circumstances.

(4) COMPLAINTS—Each audit committee shall establish procedures for—
(A) the receipt, retention, and treatment of complaints received by the issuer regarding accounting, internal accounting controls, or auditing matters; and
(B) the confidential, anonymous submission by employees of the issuer of concerns regarding questionable accounting or auditing matters.

(5) AUTHORITY TO ENGAGE ADVISORS—Each audit committee shall have the authority to engage independent counsel and other advisers, as it determines necessary to carry out its duties.

(6) FUNDING—Each issuer shall provide for appropriate funding, as determined by the audit committee, in its capacity as a committee of the board of directors, for payment of compensation—
(A) to the registered public accounting firm employed by the issuer for the purpose of rendering or issuing an audit report; and
(B) to any advisers employed by the audit committee under paragraph (5).

Action Required

Understand Section 10A (see Appendix B) and ensure compliance.

Ensure that the Audit Committee fully understands the contents of this section, and append a section to the Company's Policies and Procedures Manual describing the responsibilities of the Audit Committee.

Create procedures for complaints and anonymous concerns. (Template 3.1)

Sec. 302. Corporate responsibility for financial reports

Summary

(a) REGULATIONS REQUIRED—The Commission shall, by rule, require, for each company filing periodic reports under section 13(a) or 15(d) of the Securities Exchange Act of 1934 (15 U.S.C. 78m, 78o(d)), that the *principal executive officer or officers and the principal financial officer or officers, or persons performing similar functions, certify in each annual or quarterly report filed* or submitted under either such section of such Act that—

(1) the signing officer has *reviewed* the report;

(2) based on the officer's knowledge, the report does not contain any untrue statement of a material fact or omit to state a material fact necessary in order to make the statements made, in light of the circumstances under which such statements were made, not misleading;

(3) based on such officer's knowledge, the financial statements, and other financial information included in the report, *fairly present in all material respects the financial condition and results of operations of the issuer* as of, and for, the periods presented in the report;

(4) the signing officers—

    (A) are responsible for establishing and maintaining internal controls;

    (B) have designed such internal controls to ensure that *material information relating to the issuer and its consolidated subsidiaries is made known* to such officers by others within those entities, particularly during the period in which the periodic reports are being prepared;

    (C) have evaluated the *effectiveness of the issuer's internal controls* as of a date within 90 days prior to the report; and

    (D) have presented in the report their *conclusions about the effectiveness of their internal controls* based on their evaluation as of that date;

(5) the signing officers have disclosed to the issuer's auditors and the audit committee of the board of directors (or persons fulfilling the equivalent function)—

    (A) all significant *deficiencies in the design or operation of internal controls* which could adversely affect the issuer's ability to record, process, summarize, and report financial data and have identified for the issuer's auditors any material weaknesses in internal controls; and

    (B) *any fraud*, whether or not material, that involves management or other employees who have a significant role in the issuer's internal controls; and

(6) the signing officers have indicated in the report whether or not there were significant changes in internal controls or in other factors that could significantly affect internal controls subsequent to the date of their evaluation, including any corrective actions with

regard to significant deficiencies and material weaknesses.

(b) FOREIGN REINCORPORATIONS HAVE NO EFFECT—Nothing in this section 302 shall be interpreted or applied in any way to allow any issuer to lessen the legal force of the statement required under this section 302, by an issuer having reincorporated or having engaged in any other transaction that resulted in the transfer of the corporate domicile or offices of the issuer from inside the United States to outside of the United States.

Action Required

The kicker in this section is part (4) stating that the officers are responsible for establishing and maintaining internal controls so that any material information is available to the officers and the auditors. It is the establishment of the internal control mechanism and system that is time-consuming, expensive and detailed. Many companies have created or modified software applications to provide compliance with this requirement. Refer to Chapter 2 for an overview of Internal Control Systems and the COSO Framework used as a framework for compliance.

Include in the Policies and Procedures Manual sections outlining the officers' responsibilities in this requirement and provide approved certification templates for the CEO, CFO and other responsible officers.

(Certification Disclosure Template) Appendix D
(Internal Control Report Template) Appendix D

Sec. 303. Improper influence on conduct of audits

Summary

(a) RULES TO PROHIBIT—It shall be unlawful, in contravention of such rules or regulations as the Commission shall prescribe as necessary and appropriate in the public interest or for the protection of investors, for any officer or director of an issuer, or any other person acting under the direction thereof, to take any action to fraudulently influence, coerce, manipulate, or mislead any independent public or certified accountant engaged in the performance of an audit of the financial statements of that issuer for the purpose of rendering such financial statements materially misleading.

Action Required

Avoid any actions that could be construed as applying such influence, keep minutes of all meetings with auditors and avoid one-on-one meetings between auditor and company officers.

Transparency and accountability are the watchwords.

Sec. 304. Forfeiture of certain bonuses and profits

Summary

ADDITIONAL COMPENSATION PRIOR TO NON-COMPLIANCE WITH COMMISSION FINANCIAL REPORTING REQUIREMENTS—If an issuer is required to prepare an accounting restatement due to the material noncompliance of the issuer, as a result of misconduct, with any financial reporting requirement under the securities laws, the chief executive officer and chief financial officer of the issuer shall reimburse the issuer for—

(1) any bonus or other incentive-based or equity-based compensation received by that person from the issuer during the 12-month period following the first public issuance or filing with the Commission (whichever first occurs) of the financial document embodying such financial reporting requirement; and
(2) any profits realized from the sale of securities of the issuer during that 12-month period.

Action Required

The CFO must ensure that such reimbursements are clearly made and documented.

Sec. 305. Officer and director bars and penalties

Summary

> (1) SECURITIES EXCHANGE ACT OF 1934—Section 21(d)(2) of the Securities Exchange Act of 1934 (15 U.S.C. 78u(d)(2)) is amended by striking "substantial unfitness" and inserting "unfitness."
>
> (2) SECURITIES ACT OF 1933—Section 20(e) of the Securities Act of 1933 (15 U.S.C. 77t(e)) is amended by striking "substantial unfitness" and inserting "unfitness."
>
> (b) EQUITABLE RELIEF—Section 21(d) of the securities Exchange Act of 1934 (15 U.S.C. 78u(d)) is amended by adding at the end the following:
>
> (5) EQUITABLE RELIEF—In any action or proceeding brought or instituted by the Commission under any provision of the securities laws, the Commission may seek, and any Federal court may grant, any equitable relief that may be appropriate or necessary for the benefit of investors.

Action Required

None

Sec. 306. Insider trades during pension fund blackout periods

Summary

> IN GENERAL—Except to the extent otherwise provided by rule of the Commission pursuant to paragraph (3), it shall be unlawful for any director or executive officer of an issuer of any equity security (other than an exempted security), directly or indirectly, to purchase, sell, or otherwise acquire or transfer any equity security of the issuer (other than an exempted security) during any blackout period with respect to such equity security if such director or officer acquires such equity security in connection with his or her service or employment as a director or executive officer.

(4) BLACKOUT PERIOD—For purposes of this subsection, the term "blackout period," with respect to the equity securities of any issuer—

(A) means any period of more than 3 consecutive business days during which the ability of not fewer than 50 percent of the participants or beneficiaries under all individual account plans maintained by the issuer to purchase, sell, or otherwise acquire or transfer an interest in any equity of such issuer held in such an individual account plan is temporarily suspended by the issuer or by a fiduciary of the plan;

Action Required

Insert the appropriate prohibition in the Policies and Procedures Manual in the stock trading section. This is a complex section involving Pension Plans and the CFO must be fully cognizant of the content and implications of it.

Sec. 307. Rules of professional responsibility for attorneys

Summary

The Commission shall issue rules, in the public interest and for the protection of investors, setting forth minimum standards of professional conduct for attorneys appearing and practicing before the Commission in any way in the representation of issuers, including a rule—

(1) requiring an attorney to report evidence of a material violation of securities law or breach of fiduciary duty or similar violation by the company or any agent thereof, to the chief legal counsel or the chief executive officer of the company (or the equivalent thereof); and

(2) if the counsel or officer does not appropriately respond to the evidence (adopting, as necessary, appropriate remedial measures or sanctions with respect to the violation), requiring the attorney to report the evidence to the audit committee of the board of directors of the issuer or to another

committee of the board of directors comprised solely of directors not employed directly or indirectly by the issuer, or to the board of directors.

Action Required

None

Sec. 308. Fair funds for investors

Summary

CIVIL PENALTIES ADDED TO DISGORGEMENT FUNDS FOR THE RELIEF OF VICTIMS—If in any judicial or administrative action brought by the Commission under the securities laws (as such term is defined in section 3(a)(47) of the Securities Exchange Act of 1934 (15 U.S.C. 78c(a)(47)) the Commission obtains an order requiring disgorgement against any person for a violation of such laws or the rules or regulations thereunder, or such person agrees in settlement of any such action to such disgorgement, and the Commission also obtains pursuant to such laws a civil penalty against such person, the amount of such civil penalty shall, on the motion or at the direction of the Commission, be added to and become part of the disgorgement fund for the benefit of the victims of such violation.

Action Required

None unless an action has been brought and completed.

Title IV—Enhanced financial disclosures

Sec. 401. Disclosures in periodic reports

Summary

ACCURACY OF FINANCIAL REPORTS—Each financial report that contains financial statements, and that is required to be prepared in accordance with (or reconciled to) generally accepted accounting principles under this title and filed with the Commission shall reflect all material correcting adjustments that have been identified by a registered public accounting firm in accordance with generally accepted accounting principles and the rules and regulations of the Commission.

Action Required

Ensure that the CFO and company accounting division are fully aware of the provisions of this section and comply with all requirements. Details should be included in the Policies and Procedures Manual in the accounting and bookkeeping section(s).

Sec. 402. Enhanced conflict of interest provisions

Summary

IN GENERAL—It shall be unlawful for any issuer (as defined in section 2 of the Sarbanes–Oxley Act of 2002), directly or indirectly, including through any subsidiary, to extend or maintain credit, to arrange for the extension of credit, or to renew an extension of credit, in the form of a personal loan to or for any director or executive officer (or equivalent thereof) of that issuer. An extension of credit maintained by the issuer on the date of enactment of this subsection shall not be subject to the provisions of this subsection, provided that there is no material modification to any term of any such extension of credit or any renewal of any such extension of credit on or after that date of enactment.

Action Required

Ensure that any loans or credit to or for an officer of the company meet the requirements of this section. There are some exceptions to the prohibition, but care must be taken that any transactions of this type are clearly disclosed and transparent.

Sec. 403. Disclosures of transactions involving management and principal stockholders

Summary

> DIRECTORS, OFFICERS, AND PRINCIPAL STOCK-HOLDERS REQUIRED TO FILE—Every person who is directly or indirectly the beneficial owner of more than 10 percent of any class of any equity security (other than an exempted security) which is registered pursuant to section 12, or who is a director or an officer of the issuer of such security, shall file the statements required by this subsection with the Commission (and, if such security is registered on a national securities exchange, also with the exchange).

Action Required

Ensure that shareholders owning more than 10% of the company stock, and the directors and officers, comply with the disclosure rules of Section 16 of the SEC and that said shareholder is made aware of the provisions of this section.

Sec. 404. Management assessment of internal controls

Summary

> RULES REQUIRED—The Commission shall prescribe rules requiring each annual report required by section 13(a) or 15(d) of the Securities Exchange Act of 1934 (15 U.S.C. 78m or 78o(d)) to contain an internal control report, which shall—
>
> (1) state the responsibility of management for establishing and maintaining an adequate internal control structure and procedures for financial reporting; and

(2) contain an assessment, as of the end of the most recent fiscal year of the issuer, of the effectiveness of the internal control structure and procedures of the issuer for financial reporting.

Action Required

Create an internal control system that covers every aspect of the company's operations that affect its financial state and ensure that the system has adequate capability of issuing comprehensive and transparent reports. (see Chapter 2)

This is the tip of the iceberg. It is the section (along with 302) that requires the most effort on the part of the company. Fortunately, a variety of software solutions are available to ease the process, but compliance and detailed adherence to the application of the software used must be made the direct responsibility of a suitable officer, probably the CFO. Since the CEO is ultimately responsible, a process of reporting and assessment should be introduced to ensure that he/she is completely aware of the internal state of affairs of the company at all times. See Chapter 2 for a detailed framework (COSO) to satisfy the requirements of this Section.

Sec. 405. Exemption

Summary

> Nothing in section 401, 402, or 404, the amendments made by those sections, or the rules of the Commission under those sections shall apply to any investment company registered under section 8 of the Investment Company Act of 1940 (1 U.S.C. 80a-8).

Action Required

None

Sec. 406. Code of ethics for senior financial officers

Summary

> CODE OF ETHICS DISCLOSURE—The Commission shall issue rules to require each issuer, together with

periodic reports required pursuant to section 13(a) or 15(d) of the Securities Exchange Act of 1934, to disclose whether or not, and if not, the reason therefore, such issuer has adopted a code of ethics for senior financial officers, applicable to its principal financial officer and comptroller or principal accounting officer, or persons performing similar functions.

Action Required

Generate a suitable Code of Ethics and insert it in the Policies and Procedures Manual. Ensure that the CFO and other financial officers are aware of it, sign it, and agree to abide by it. (see Appendix D)

Sec. 407. Disclosure of audit committee financial expert

Summary

The Commission shall issue rules, as necessary or appropriate in the public interest and consistent with the protection of investors, to require each issuer, together with periodic reports required pursuant to sections 13(a) and 15(d) of the Securities Exchange Act of 1934, to disclose whether or not, and if not, the reasons therefore, the audit committee of that issuer is comprised of at least 1 member who is a financial expert, as such term is defined by the Commission.

Action Required

Ensure that at least one member of the Audit Committee meets the requirements.

Sec. 408. Enhanced review of periodic disclosures by issuers

Summary

The Commission shall review disclosures made by issuers reporting under section 13(a) of the Securities Exchange Act of 1934 (including reports filed on Form 10-K), and which have a class of securities listed on a national securities exchange or traded on an automated quotation facility of a national securities association, on a regular and systematic basis for the protection of investors. Such review shall include a review of an issuer's financial statement.

Action Required

None

Sec. 409. Real time issuer disclosures

Summary

Each issuer reporting under section 13(a) or 15(d) shall disclose to the public on a rapid and current basis such additional information concerning material changes in the financial condition or operations of the issuer, in plain English, which may include trend and qualitative information and graphic presentations, as the Commission determines, by rule, is necessary or useful for the protection of investors and in the public interest.

Action Required

In addition to the Annual Report, and/or Quarterly Reports, provide a medium for disseminating such relevant information to shareholders and the public, such as a Newsletter, Press Releases or on the company website. Appoint an officer to ensure that any such relevant information is promptly disseminated.

Title V—Analyst conflicts of interest

Sec. 501. Treatment of securities analysts by registered securities associations and national securities exchanges

Summary

ANALYST PROTECTIONS—The Commission, or upon the authorization and direction of the Commission, a registered securities association or national securities exchange, shall have adopted, not later than 1 year after the date of enactment of this section, rules reasonably designed to address conflicts of interest that can arise when securities analysts recommend equity securities in research reports and public appearances, in order to improve the objectivity of research and provide investors with more useful and reliable information.

Action Required

Essentially there should be no relationship between the broker and the company that may be perceived as a conflict of interest. No debts or financial interest other than the normal brokerage commissions.

Title VI—Commission resources and authority

Sec. 601. Authorization of appropriations

Summary

In addition to any other funds authorized to be appropriated to the Commission, there are authorized to be appropriated to carry out the functions, powers, and duties of the Commission, $776,000,000 for fiscal year 2003.

Action Required

None

Sec. 602. Appearance and practice before the Commission

Summary

AUTHORITY TO CENSURE—The Commission may censure any person, or deny, temporarily or permanently, to any person the privilege of appearing or practicing before the Commission in any way, if that person is found by the Commission, after notice and opportunity for hearing in the matter—

(1) not to possess the requisite qualifications to represent others;
(2) to be lacking in character or integrity, or to have engaged in unethical or improper professional conduct; or
(3) to have willfully violated, or willfully aided and abetted the violation of, any provision of the securities laws or the rules and regulations issued thereunder.

Action Required

If there is a need to appear before the commission for any reason, ensure the person(s) appearing meet the criteria above.

Sec. 603. Federal court authority to impose penny stock bars

Summary

> IN GENERAL—In any proceeding under paragraph (1) against any person participating in, or, at the time of the alleged misconduct who was participating in, an offering of penny stock, the court may prohibit that person from participating in an offering of penny stock, conditionally or unconditionally, and permanently or for such period of time as the court shall determine.

Action Required

None unless the situation arises

Sec. 604. Qualifications of associated persons of brokers and dealers

Summary

> BROKERS AND DEALERS—Section 15(b)(4) of the Securities Exchange Act of 1934 (15 U.S.C. 78o) is amended—
>
> (1) by striking subparagraph (F) and inserting the following:
>
> (F) is subject to any order of the Commission barring or suspending the right of the person to be associated with a broker or dealer; and
>
> (2) in subparagraph (G), by striking the period at the end and inserting the following: or
>
> (H) is subject to any final order of a State securities commission (or any agency or officer performing like functions), State authority that supervises or examines banks, savings associations, or credit unions, State insurance commission (or any agency or office performing like functions), an appropriate

Federal banking agency (as defined in section 3 of the Federal Deposit Insurance Act (12 U.S.C. 1813(q)), or the National Credit Union Administration, that—

(i) bars such person from association with an entity regulated by such commission, authority, agency, or officer, or from engaging in the business of securities, insurance, banking, saving association activities, or credit union activities;

Action Required

None by the company, but ensure associated brokers and dealers are in compliance.

Title VII—Studies and reports

Sec. 701. GAO study and report regarding consolidation of public accounting firms

Summary

(a) STUDY REQUIRED—The Comptroller General of the United States shall conduct a study—

(1) to identify—

(A) the factors that have led to the consolidation of public accounting firms since 1989 and the consequent reduction in the number of firms capable of providing audit services to large national and multi-national business organizations that are subject to the securities laws;

(B) the present and future impact of the condition described in subparagraph (A) on capital formation and securities markets, both domestic and international; and

(C) solutions to any problems identified under subparagraph (B), including ways to increase competition and the number of firms capable of providing audit services to large national and multinational business organizations that are subject to the securities laws;

(2) of the problems, if any, faced by business organizations that have resulted from limited competition among public accounting firms, including—

(A) higher costs;

(B) lower quality of services;

(C) impairment of auditor independence; or

(D) lack of choice; and

(3) whether and to what extent Federal or State regulations impede competition among public accounting firms.

(b) CONSULTATION—In planning and conducting the study under this section, the Comptroller General shall consult with—

(1) the Commission;

(2) the regulatory agencies that perform functions similar to the Commission within the other member countries of the Group of Seven Industrialized Nations;

(3) the Department of Justice; and

(4) any other public or private sector organization that the Comptroller General considers appropriate.

Action Required

None

Sec. 702. Commission study and report regarding credit rating agencies

Summary

IN GENERAL—The Commission shall conduct a study of the role and function of credit rating agencies in the operation of the securities market.

AREAS OF CONSIDERATION—The study required by this subsection shall examine—

(A) the role of credit rating agencies in the evaluation of issuers of securities;

(B) the importance of that role to investors and the functioning of the securities markets;

(C) any impediments to the accurate appraisal by credit rating agencies of the financial resources and risks of issuers of securities;

(D) any barriers to entry into the business of acting as a credit rating agency, and any measures needed to remove such barriers;

(E) any measures which may be required to improve the dissemination of information concerning such resources and risks when credit rating agencies announce credit ratings; and

(F) any conflicts of interest in the operation of credit rating agencies and measures to prevent such conflicts or ameliorate the consequences of such conflicts.

Action Required

None

Sec. 703. Study and report on violators and violations

Summary

STUDY—The Commission shall conduct a study to determine, based upon information for the period from January 1, 1998, to December 31, 2001—

(1) the number of securities professionals, defined as public accountants, public accounting firms, investment bankers, investment advisers, brokers, dealers, attorneys, and other securities professionals practicing before the Commission—

(A) who have been found to have aided and abetted a violation of the Federal securities laws, including rules or regulations promulgated thereunder (collectively referred to in this section as "Federal securities laws"), but who have not been sanctioned, disciplined, or otherwise penalized as a primary violator in an administrative action or civil proceeding, including in any settlement of such an action or proceeding (referred to in this section as "aiders and abettors"); and

(B) who have been found to have been primary violators of the Federal securities laws;

(2) a description of the Federal securities laws violations committed by aiders and abettors and by primary violators, including—

(A) the specific provision of the Federal securities laws violated;

(B) the specific sanctions and penalties imposed upon such aiders and abettors and primary violators, including the amount of any monetary penalties assessed upon and collected from such persons;

(C) the occurrence of multiple violations by the same person or persons, either as an aider or abettor or as a primary violator; and

(D) whether, as to each such violator, disciplinary sanctions have been imposed, including any censure, suspension, temporary bar, or permanent bar to practice before the Commission; and (3) the amount of disgorgement, restitution, or any other fines or payments that the Commission has assessed upon and collected from, aiders and abettors and from primary violators.

Action Required

None

Sec. 704. Study of enforcement actions

Summary

STUDY REQUIRED—The Commission shall review and analyze all enforcement actions by the Commission involving violations of reporting requirements imposed under the securities laws, and restatements of financial statements, over the 5-year period preceding the date of enactment of this Act, to identify areas of reporting that are most susceptible to fraud, inappropriate manipulation, or inappropriate earnings management, such as revenue recognition and the accounting treatment of off-balance sheet special purpose entities.

Action Required

None

Sec. 705. Study of investment banks

Summary

GAO STUDY—The Comptroller General of the United States shall conduct a study on whether investment banks and financial advisers assisted public companies in manipulating their earnings and obfuscating their true financial condition.

Action Required

None

Title VIII—Corporate and criminal fraud accountability

Sec. 801. Short title

Summary

> This title may be cited as the "Corporate and Criminal Fraud Accountability Act of 2002."

Action Required

None

Sec. 802. Criminal penalties for altering documents

Summary

> IN GENERAL—Chapter 73 of title 18, United States Code, is amended by adding at the end the following:
>
> §1519. Destruction, alteration, or falsification of records in Federal investigations and bankruptcy
>
> "Whoever knowingly alters, destroys, mutilates, conceals, covers up, falsifies, or makes a false entry in any record, document, or tangible object with the intent to impede, obstruct, or influence the investigation or proper administration of any matter within the jurisdiction of any department or agency of the United States or any case filed under title 11, or in relation to or contemplation of any such matter or case, shall be fined under this title, imprisoned not more than 20 years, or both."

Action Required

Put in place a system for filing and locating any and all documentation and records of the company including memos and e-mails relating to company business or operations. Basically, anything affecting the company must be retained and accessible.

Sec. 803. Debts non-dischargeable if incurred in violation of securities fraud laws

Summary

Section 523(a) of title 11, United States Code, is amended—

(1) in paragraph (17), by striking "or" after the semicolon;

(2) in paragraph (18), by striking the period at the end and inserting "; or"; and

(3) by adding at the end, the following: "(19) that—

(A) is for—

   (i) the violation of any of the Federal securities laws (as that term is defined in section 3(a)(47) of the Securities Exchange Act of 1934), any of the State securities laws, or any regulation or order issued under such Federal or State securities laws; or

   (ii) common law fraud, deceit, or manipulation in connection with the purchase or sale of any security; and

(B) results from—

   (i) any judgment, order, consent order, or decree entered in any Federal or State judicial or administrative proceeding;

   (ii) any settlement agreement entered into by the debtor; or

   (iii) any court or administrative order for any damages, fine, penalty, citation, restitutionary payment, disgorgement payment, attorney fee, cost, or other payment owed by the debtor."

Action Required

None

Sec. 804. Statute of limitations for securities fraud

Summary

IN GENERAL—Section 1658 of title 28, United States Code, is amended—

(1) by inserting "(a)" before "Except"; and

(2) by adding at the end the following:

(b) Notwithstanding subsection (a), a private right of action that involves a claim of fraud, deceit, manipulation, or contrivance in contravention of a regulatory requirement concerning the securities laws, as defined in section 3(a)(47) of the Securities Exchange Act of 1934 (15 U.S.C. 78c(a)(47)), may be brought not later than the earlier of—

(1) 2 years after the discovery of the facts constituting the violation; or

(2) 5 years after such violation.

EFFECTIVE DATE—The limitations period provided by section 1658(b) of title 28, United States Code, as added by this section, shall apply to all proceedings addressed by this section that are commenced on or after the date of enactment of this Act.

(c) NO CREATION OF ACTIONS—Nothing in this section shall create a new, private right of action.

Action Required

None

Sec. 805. Review of Federal Sentencing Guidelines for obstruction of justice and extensive criminal fraud

Summary

ENHANCEMENT OF FRAUD AND OBSTRUCTION OF JUSTICE SENTENCES—Pursuant to section 994 of title 28, United States Code, and in accordance with this section, the United States Sentencing Commission shall review and amend, as appropriate, the Federal Sentencing Guidelines and related policy statements to ensure that—

(1) the base offense level and existing enhancements contained in United States Sentencing Guideline 2J1.2 relating to obstruction of justice are sufficient to deter and punish that activity;

(2) the enhancements . . .

Action Required

None

Sec. 806. Protection for employees of publicly traded companies who provide evidence of fraud

Summary

WHISTLEBLOWER PROTECTION FOR EMPLOYEES OF PUBLICLY TRADED COMPANIES—No company with a class of securities registered under section 12 of the Securities Exchange Act of 1934 (15 U.S.C. 78l), or that is required to file reports under section 15(d) of the Securities Exchange Act of 1934 (15 U.S.C. 78o(d)), or any officer, employee, contractor, subcontractor, or agent of such company, may discharge, demote, suspend, threaten, harass, or in any other manner discriminate against an employee in the terms and conditions of employment because of any lawful act done by the employee—

(1) to provide information, cause information to be provided, or otherwise assist in an investigation regarding any conduct which the employee reasonably believes constitutes a violation of section 1341, 1343, 1344, or 1348, any rule or regulation of the Securities and Exchange Commission, or any provision of Federal law relating to fraud against shareholders, when the information or assistance is provided to or the investigation is conducted by—

(A) a Federal regulatory or law enforcement agency;

(B) any Member of Congress or any committee of Congress; or

(C) a person with supervisory authority over the employee (or such other person working for the employer who has the authority to investigate, discover, or terminate misconduct); or

(2) to file, cause to be filed, testify, participate in, or otherwise assist in a proceeding filed or about to be filed (with any knowledge of the employer) relating to an alleged violation of section 1341, 1343, 1344, or 1348, any rule or regulation of the Securities and Exchange Commission, or any provision of Federal law relating to fraud against shareholders.

Action Required

Create a system whereby an employee can report or provide information anonymously to the officers of the company, the Board and particularly the Audit Committee so that problems and violations can be remedied internally. Employees must believe they will not be punished or otherwise adversely affected by such disclosures to the company. (Template 3.1)

Sec. 807. Criminal penalties for defrauding shareholders of publicly traded companies

Summary

1348. Securities fraud

Whoever knowingly executes, or attempts to execute, a scheme or artifice—

(1) to defraud any person in connection with any security of an issuer with a class of securities registered under section 12 of the Securities Exchange Act of 1934 (15 U.S.C. 78l) or that is required to file reports under section 15(d) of the Securities Exchange Act of 1934 (15 U.S.C. 78o(d)); or

(2) to obtain, by means of false or fraudulent pretenses, representations, or promises, any money or property in connection with the purchase or sale of any security of an issuer with a class of

securities registered under section 12 of the Securities Exchange Act of 1934 (15 U.S.C. 78l) or that is required to file reports under section 15(d) of the Securities Exchange Act of 1934 (15 U.S.C. 78o(d)); shall be fined under this title, or imprisoned not more than 25 years, or both.

Action Required

None, other than obtaining legal counsel regarding the issuance of shares and the documentation pertaining to the issuance, such as the IPO, etc.

Title IX—White-Collar crime penalty enhancements

Sec. 901. Short title

Summary

This title may be cited as the "White-Collar Crime Penalty Enhancement Act of 2002."

Action Required

None

Sec. 902. Attempts and conspiracies to commit criminal fraud offenses

Summary

IN GENERAL—Chapter 63 of title 18, United States Code, is amended by inserting after section 1348 as added by this Act the following:

§1349. Attempt and conspiracy

"Any person who attempts or conspires to commit any offense under this chapter shall be subject to the same penalties as those prescribed for the offense, the commission of which was the object of the attempt or conspiracy."

Action Required

None

Sec. 903. Criminal penalties for mail and wire fraud

Summary

(a) MAIL FRAUD—Section 1341 of title 18, United States Code, is amended by striking "five" and inserting "20".

(b) WIRE FRAUD—Section 1343 of title 18, United States Code, is amended by striking "five" and inserting "20".

Action Required

None

Sec. 904. Criminal penalties for violations of the Employee Retirement Income Security Act of 1974

Summary

> Section 501 of the Employee Retirement Income Security Act of 1974 (29 U.S.C. 1131) is amended—
> (1) by striking "$5,000" and inserting "$100,000";
> (2) by striking "one year" and inserting "10 years"; and
> (3) by striking "$100,000" and inserting "$500,000".

Action Required

None

Sec. 905. Amendment to sentencing guidelines relating to certain white-collar offenses

Summary

> DIRECTIVE TO THE UNITED STATES SENTENCING COMMISSION—Pursuant to its authority under section 994(p) of title 18, United States Code, and in accordance with this section, the United States Sentencing Commission shall review and, as appropriate, amend the Federal Sentencing Guidelines and related policy statements to implement the provisions of this Act.

Action Required

None

Sec. 906. Corporate responsibility for financial reports

Summary

> 1350. Failure of corporate officers to certify financial reports
>
> (a) CERTIFICATION OF PERIODIC FINANCIAL REPORTS—Each periodic report containing financial statements filed by an issuer with the Securities Exchange Commission pursuant to section 13(a) or 15(d) of the Securities Exchange

Act of 1934 (15 U.S.C. 78m(a) or 78o(d)) shall be accompanied by a written statement by the chief executive officer and chief financial officer (or equivalent thereof) of the issuer.

(b) CONTENT—The statement required under subsection (a) shall certify that the periodic report containing the financial statements fully complies with the requirements of section 13(a) or 15(d) of the Securities Exchange Act of 1934 (15 U.S.C. 78m or 78o(d)) and that information contained in the periodic report fairly presents, in all material respects, the financial condition and results of operations of the issuer.

Action Required

Produce report templates to cover the requirements of this section for the CFO and CEO. The fact that both the CFO and the CEO will be held liable for any errors or omissions in the financial reports which could result in heavy fines ($1,000,000 or $5,000,000 if willful) and possibly jail sentences (10 to 20 years) suggests that a process be initiated in the company such that the CEO and the CFO (who should be fully cognizant anyway) are able to review the pertinent reports against the financial and other records of the company in an easily understood manner. In a small company this should not be difficult but in a large one, the CEO will be taking a risk if he/she simply relies on others to validate the reports and then signs them off. Ensure that the certifications comply with the SEA items mentioned.

Title X—Corporate tax returns

Sec. 1001. Sense of the Senate regarding the signing of corporate tax returns by chief executive officers

Summary

> It is the sense of the Senate that the Federal income tax return of a corporation should be signed by the chief executive officer of such corporation.

Action Required

Since the CEO will sign the return it follows that he/she must be fully cognizant of its content and accuracy. Since these returns are often complex, a CEO is going to have a lot of confidence and trust in his/her CFO. Otherwise, it may be desirable to have a third party evaluate the return on behalf of the CEO before he/she signs it.

Title XI—Corporate fraud and accountability

Sec. 1101. Short title

Summary

> This title may be cited as the "Corporate Fraud Accountability Act of 2002."

Action Required

None

Sec. 1102. Tampering with a record or otherwise impeding an official proceeding

Summary

> Whoever corruptly—
> (1) alters, destroys, mutilates, or conceals a record, document, or other object, or attempts to do so, with the intent to impair the object's integrity or availability for use in an official proceeding; or
> (2) otherwise obstructs, influences, or impedes any official proceeding, or attempts to do so, shall be fined under this title or imprisoned not more than 20 years, or both.

Action Required

See section 802 and then also enter a section in the company Policies and Procedures Manual concerning maintaining the integrity of documents and reports as they pass through various hands in the company, in particular by initialing and dating handling of significant documents that may be required in an investigation.

Sec. 1103. Temporary freeze authority for the Securities and Exchange Commission

Summary

> IN GENERAL—
> (i) ISSUANCE OF TEMPORARY ORDER—Whenever, during the course of a lawful investigation involving possible violations of the Federal securities

laws by an issuer of publicly traded securities or any of its directors, officers, partners, controlling persons, agents, or employees, it shall appear to the Commission that it is likely that the issuer will make extraordinary payments (whether compensation or otherwise) to any of the foregoing persons, the Commission may petition a Federal district court for a temporary order requiring the issuer to escrow, subject to court supervision, those payments in an interest-bearing account for 45 days.

Action Required

None

Sec. 1104. Amendment to the Federal Sentencing Guidelines

Summary

REQUEST FOR IMMEDIATE CONSIDERATION BY THE UNITED STATES SENTENCING COMMISSION—Pursuant to its authority under section 994(p) of title 28, United States Code, and in accordance with this section, the United States Sentencing Commission is requested to—

(1) promptly review the sentencing guidelines applicable to securities and accounting fraud and related offenses;

(2) expeditiously consider the promulgation of new sentencing guidelines or amendments to existing sentencing guidelines to provide an enhancement for officers or directors of publicly traded corporations who commit fraud and related offenses; and

(3) submit to Congress an explanation of actions taken by the Sentencing Commission pursuant to paragraph (2) and any additional policy recommendations the Sentencing Commission may have for combating offenses described in paragraph (1).

Action Required

None

Sec. 1105. Authority of the Commission to prohibit persons from serving as officers or directors

Summary

AUTHORITY OF THE COMMISSION TO PROHIBIT PERSONS FROM SERVING AS OFFICERS OR DIRECTORS—In any cease-and-desist proceeding under subsection (a), the Commission may issue an order to prohibit, conditionally or unconditionally, and permanently or for such period of time as it shall determine, any person who has violated section 10(b) or the rules or regulations thereunder, from acting as an officer or director of any issuer that has a class of securities registered pursuant to section 12, or that is required to file reports pursuant to section 15(d), if the conduct of that person demonstrates unfitness to serve as an officer or director of any such issuer.

Action Required

None

Sec. 1106. Increased criminal penalties under Securities Exchange Act of 1934

Summary

Section 32(a) of the Securities Exchange Act of 1934 (15 U.S.C. 78ff(a)) is amended—
(1) by striking "$1,000,000, or imprisoned not more than 10 years" and inserting "$5,000,000, or imprisoned not more than 20 years"; and
(2) by striking "$2,500,000" and inserting "$25,000,000".

Action Required

None

Sec. 1107. Retaliation against informants

Summary

IN GENERAL—Section 1513 of title 18, United States Code, is amended by adding at the end the following:

"(e) Whoever knowingly, with the intent to retaliate, takes any action harmful to any person, including interference with the lawful employment or livelihood of any person, for providing to a law enforcement officer any truthful information relating to the commission or possible commission of any Federal offense, shall be fined under this title or imprisoned not more than 10 years, or both."

Action Required

Ensure that all supervisors and managers are aware of this provision, and enter it in the Policies and Procedures Manual.

The Internal Control System

A framework for enterprise risk management

PricewaterhouseCoopers has authored a draft *Enterprise Risk Management Framework* for the Committee of Sponsoring Organizations of the Treadway Commission (COSO). The draft framework provides a benchmark for organizations to consider in evaluating and improving their enterprise risk management processes.

While there has been much written regarding enterprise risk management, COSO determined there is a need for a broadly accepted framework for enterprise risk management. The project includes a comprehensive validation process with the draft framework being widely circulated for comment prior to being finalized by PricewaterhouseCoopers on behalf of COSO.

The COSO Framework was released in late September 2004. It appears that this framework will be the one most widely used by companies when setting up their internal controls (disclosure controls) system. To date there are a number of software systems available from private software development companies that can provide the basis for a company's system. The price of these systems varies widely and thorough research is required to find the one most suitable for a given company.

Chapter 2 contains an overview of the COSO Framework July 2004 edition* as released in September 2004. I appreciate their permission to quote at length from their document. Copies of the entire document can be obtained from the American Institute of Certified Public Accountants. www.aicpa.org. This Manual is intended to provide an idea of the scope and structure of the Sarbanes–Oxley compliance requirements, but it is essential that a company or corporation implementing a program of compliance obtain either an up-to-date and reliable software package, or a detailed copy of the COSO Framework or similar document.

The establishment of a comprehensive Internal Control system is necessary to comply with the requirements of sections 302 and 404 of the Act. It is not an easy or inexpensive project and will require the cooperation of management and department heads working with the accounting department to create a useful and compliant structure.

---

* Copyright 1992, 1994 Committee of Sponsoring Organizations of the Treadway Commission.

Subsequently, it requires the cooperation and involvement of every individual in a company to make the system work effectively and accurately. The benefits of creating the system will extend well beyond satisfying the SOX requirements, and could more than compensate for the time and effort expended in increased efficiency, accountability, and awareness of the company's operations.

There are a number of terms used by different organizations that all refer to more or less the same problems and solutions. They include "Corporate Governance", "Enterprise Risk Management", "Internal Control System", and "Disclosure Controls."

In this manual we will use the term "Internal Control System" except where we are quoting a third party.

Internal control: a definition

A process, effected by an entity's board of directors, management and other personnel, designed to provide reasonable assurance regarding the achievement of objectives in the following *categories*.

(a) Effectiveness and efficiency of operations (*Operations*)
(b) Reliability of financial reporting (*Financial Reporting*)
(c) Compliance with applicable laws and regulations. (*Compliance*)

The Structure

The *components* of the Internal Control (IC) structure are those required to provide the necessary environment to satisfy the foregoing process.

(a) The *Control Environment* provides the atmosphere in a company in which people conduct their activities and carry out their control responsibilities. It is the essential foundation for the other elements, or components.
(b) The *Risk Assessment* function is where management assesses the risks associated with achievement of specific objectives.
(c) *Control Activities* are implemented to help ensure that management directives to address the identified risks are carried out.
(d) A system of *Information and Communication* ensures that everyone is informed concerning relevant matters throughout the organization.

(e) The entire process is *monitored* and consequently modified if necessary.

To summarize, the structure is built and maintained, using these elements, to enable the Internal Control process objectives to be achieved. Remember there are three categories:

(a) Operations
(b) Financial Reporting
(c) Compliance

And five components:

(1) Control Environment
(2) Risk Assessment
(3) Control Activities
(4) Information and Communication
(5) Monitoring.

The following is a diagram from the COSO Internal Controls document. It shows neatly the elements involved in the Internal Control environment.

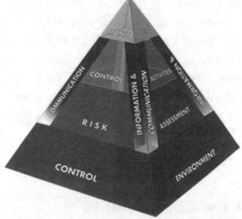

Internal Control Components

The *control environment* provides an atmosphere in which people conduct their activities and carry out their control responsibilities. It serves as the foundation for the other components. Within this environment, management *assesses risks* to the achievement of specified objectives. *Control activities* are implemented to help ensure that management directives to address the risks are carried out. Meanwhile, relevant *information* is captured and *communicated* throughout the organization. The entire process is *monitored* and modified as conditions warrant.

Courtesy of COSO

Effectiveness

The Internal Control system can be judged to be effective in each of the three categories, "Operations," "Financial Reporting," and "Compliance," when the board of directors and management have reasonable assurance that:

(a) They understand the extent to which the company's operations objectives are being achieved.
(b) Published financial statements are being prepared reliably and accurately.
(c) Applicable laws and regulations are being complied with.

The success of the entire IC structure relies on the components being applied diligently in each department (or operational entity) within an organization. Typically a department head will be responsible for ensuring that the components are applied in the three categories in his or her department. If they all do so, then the board and management can be reasonably assured that the system is effective as described above.

Evaluation

It is important that the components and elements of the internal control system as described here be evaluated by a knowledge-able, competent and independent evaluator. It can be someone within the company, an auditor, director or external consultant, but he or she must be permitted to make a comprehensive and uninfluenced evaluation, and report the results to the board of directors and audit committee as well as to management. Depending on the size of the organization, this function may be performed by a single "Internal Auditor" or by an **"Internal Audit Committee."**

Discussion of the Components

The Control Environment

The Control Environment sets the tone of the entire organization, influencing the control consciousness of its people. It is the foundation for all other components of internal control, providing discipline and structure. Control environment factors include the integrity, ethical values and competence of the entity's people; management's philosophy and operating style; the way management assigns authority and responsibility, and organizes and develops its people; and the attention and direction provided by the board of directors.(COSO)

The Control Environment encompasses the following factors.

Integrity and Ethical Values:

(a) Incentives and Temptations – reasonable expectations and targets.
(b) Providing and communicating moral guidance – people imitate their leaders.
(c) Commitment to Competence – match the individual to the job.

Board of Directors and Audit Committee.

(a) Independence from Management – some outside directors
(b) Experience and Stature – expertise and integrity
(c) Extent of Involvement – question and scrutinize
(d) Appropriateness of Actions – fairness and consistency, effectiveness.

Management's Philosophy and Operating Style:

(a) Attitudes Towards Financial Reporting – conservative or aggressive
(b) Business Attitudes – conservative or adventurous
(c) Management Style – formal or casual

Organizational Structure:

(a) Appropriateness – matched to the size and nature of the business
(b) Assignment of Authority and Responsibility
(c) Delegation and Accountability – central control or frontline decision-making.

Human Resource Policies and Practices:

(a) Hiring Policies – experience, competence, behavior, integrity
(b) Hiring Practices – interviews, presentations of company policies, goals.
(c) Promotions – performance based, available.
(d) Compensation – bonus incentives

(e) Discipline – penalties for violations of expected behavior

(f) Training and Education – ongoing process.

These elements of the Control Environment are shown here in point form to alert management to the areas that need to be addressed. The COSO Internal Controls document goes into each element thoroughly. It is also apparent that a well thought out and written Policies and Procedures Manual must be maintained by the company and read by its people. How well these concepts, expectations and rules are presented will in large measure influence the attitudes and behavior of everyone in the company.

Risk Assessment

> Every entity faces a variety of risks from external and internal sources that must be assessed. A precondition to risk assessment is establishment of objectives, linked at different levels and internally consistent. Risk assessment is the identification and analysis of relevant risks to achievement of the objectives, forming a basis for determining how the risks should be managed. Because economic, industry, regulatory and operating conditions will continue to change, mechanisms are needed to identify and deal with the special risks associated with change.(COSO)

Objective setting is a precondition for risk assessment. While not in itself a component of Internal Control it needs to be considered.

Objective Setting:

(a) Entity-level Objectives – strategic plan, business plan, mission statement.

(b) Activity-level Objectives – specific goals, integrated, measurable.

(c) Categories of Objectives – Operations. Financial Reporting, Compliance.

(d) Linkage – consistent, complementary, prioritized.

(e) Achievement – Expectations. consistent, complementary, prioritized.

Risks:

(a) Risk Identification – internal and external factors entity level, activity level.

(b) Risk Analysis – significance, likelihood, action options.

Change Management:

(a) Identifying Change – capture, process, report. Circumstances requiring special attention –
   (1) Changed Operating Environment
   (2) New Personnel
   (3) New or Revamped Information Systems
   (4) Rapid Growth
   (5) New Technology
   (6) New Lines, Products, Activities
   (7) Corporate Restructuring
   (8) Foreign Operations
(b) Mechanisms:
   Identify Changes – risks, opportunities, action plans, implementation, evaluation.
   Forward Looking Significant Changes – anticipation, avoidance, early warning system.

Control Activities

Control Activities are the policies and procedures that help ensure management directives are carried out. They help ensure that necessary actions are taken to address risks to achievement of the entity's objectives. Control activities occur throughout the organization, at all levels and in all functions. They include a range of activities as diverse as approvals, authorizations, verifications, reconciliations, reviews of operating performance, security of assets and segregation of duties.(COSO)

Types of Control Activities:

(a) Top Level Reviews – actual performance v projections, forecasts
(b) Functional or Activity Management – review performance reports, reconciliations
(c) Information Processing – accuracy, completeness, authorization of transactions, tracking.
(d) Physical Controls – equipment, securities, cash and inventory control
(e) Performance Indicators – analyze relationship of operating and financial data sets, trends, results
(f) Segregation of Duties – delegation, appropriate responsibilities, division of responsibility.

Policies and Procedures:

(a) Policies – what should be done

(b) Procedures – how to effect the policies

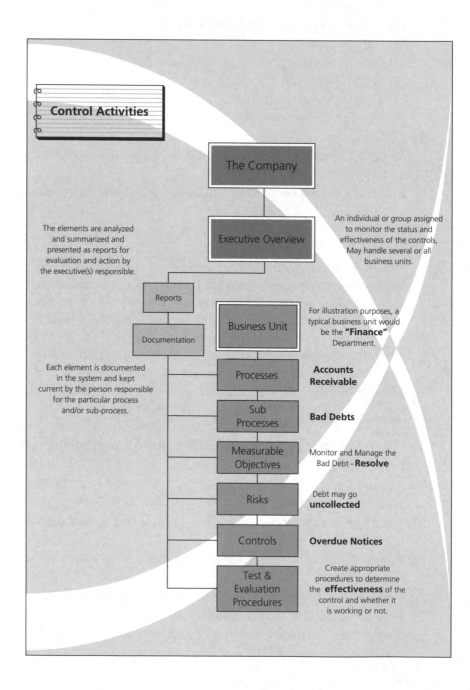

Control Activities

The Company

Executive Overview

An individual or group assigned to monitor the status and effectiveness of the controls, May handle several or all business units.

The elements are analyzed and summarized and presented as reports for evaluation and action by the executive(s) responsible.

Reports

Documentation

Business Unit

For illustration purposes, a typical business unit would be the **"Finance"** Department.

Each element is documented in the system and kept current by the person responsible for the particular process and/or sub-process.

Processes — **Accounts Receivable**

Sub Processes — **Bad Debts**

Measurable Objectives — Monitor and Manage the Bad Debt–**Resolve**

Risks — Debt may go **uncollected**

Controls — **Overdue Notices**

Test & Evaluation Procedures — Create appropriate procedures to determine the **effectiveness** of the control and whether it is working or not.

Note: A comprehensive, up-to-date and easily followed company Policies and Procedures Manual is a vital tool for maintaining coherent and consistent activities within the company, no matter how small or simple the company is.

Integration with Risk Management:

(a) Identify – identify and describe the actions needed to address the risks
(b) Actions – take the necessary actions to mitigate or control the risks identified

Note: Wherever third party confirmation of the company's compliance is required, or other relevant advice or material information is needed, obtain the confirmation and information in writing. A valid and auditable paper trail is at the heart of this whole exercise.

Controls over Information Systems:

GENERAL CONTROLS

Includes controls over data center operations, system software acquisition and maintenance, access security, privacy controls, application system development and maintenance.

(a) Data Center Operations Controls – job set-up and scheduling, operator actions, backup and recovery procedures, contingency and disaster recovery planning.
(b) System Software Controls – acquisition, implementation, maintenance, logging, tracking, monitoring.
(c) Access Security Controls – protect unauthorized access, inappropriate use of the system.
(d) Privacy Controls – protection of data from unauthorized access and manipulation.
(e) Application System Development and Maintenance Controls – structure and methodology.

APPLICATION CONTROLS

Processing Controls – ensure completeness and accuracy, authorization and validity, ongoing data checks, operator training.

The General and Application controls are interrelated and it is apparent that the corporate systems must be acquired, designed and structured so that they work seamlessly together, which is a General Control function, and that the system(s) used provide the means for controlling the accuracy and validity of the data input, the Application Control function. Different departments or entities may require different solutions, but they must be compatible and capable of communicating with each other as well as producing usable reports.

Information and Communication

> Pertinent information must be identified, captured and communicated in a form and timeframe that enables people to carry out their responsibilities. Information systems produce reports containing operational, financial and compliance related information that make it possible to run and control the business. They deal not only with internally generated data, but also information about external events, activities and conditions necessary to informed business decision making and external reporting. Effective communication also must occur in a broader sense, flowing down, across and up the organization. All personnel must receive a clear message from top management that control responsibilities must be taken seriously. They must understand their own role in the internal control system, as well as how individual activities relate to the work of others. They must have a means of communicating significant information upstream. There also needs to be effective communication with external parties such as customers, suppliers, regulators and shareholders.(COSO)

Information

Information is necessary throughout the organization in order to attain the objectives of the three categories, operations, financial reporting and compliance.

Strategic and Integrated Systems:

(a) Systems Support Strategic Initiatives – suitable off-the-shelf, customizable or internally designed systems employed to carry out the strategic objectives of a company.
(b) Integration with Operations – various systems are integrated to facilitate tracking and control of the company's activities.
(c) Coexisting Technologies – choose and use the information technologies that do the job best, not necessarily the newest.
(d) Information Quality – appropriate, timely, current, accurate, accessible.

Communication

Information is only useful when it can be communicated to the appropriate personnel to enable them to perform their duties and help them achieve their objectives.

(a) Internal – Objectives and needs are clearly communicated down through the organization and performance reports, problems and ideas communicate upwards. Open channels not just to supervisors but to senior management (without reprisal).
(b) External – Relevant information flows outwards to suppliers, regulators, shareholders and customers, while new product information, problems, rules and procedures are communicated back to the organization.
(c) Means of Communication – policy manuals, memoranda, bulletin boards, newsletters, e-mail and meetings. Brochures, reports, presentations, advertisements.

A highly important means of communication is the behavior and attitudes of management. Honesty, integrity and fairness as a way of doing business and dealing with employees, customers and suppliers will be reflected all the way throughout the company.

Monitoring

> Internal Control Systems need to be monitored – a process that assesses the quality of the system's performance over time. This is accomplished through ongoing monitoring activities, separate evaluations or a combination of the two. Ongoing monitoring occurs in the course of operations. It includes regular management and supervisory activities, and other actions personnel take in performing their duties. The scope and frequency of separate evaluations will depend primarily on an assessment of risks and the effectiveness of ongoing monitoring procedures. Internal control deficiencies should be reported upstream, with serious matters reported to top management and the board.(COSO)

Ongoing Monitoring Activities

Ongoing monitoring procedures are built into the normal, recurring activities of an entity. Because they are performed on a real-time basis, they are more effective than separate evaluations in their ability to identify problems quickly. Examples are:

(a) *Reports:* When operating reports are integrated with the financial reporting system and used to manage operations on an ongoing basis, significant inaccuracies or exceptions to anticipated results are likely to be spotted quickly. The effectiveness of the Internal Control System is enhanced by timely, complete and accurate reporting, and subsequent actions resolving exceptions.

(b) *External Communications:* Communications from customers, clients, insurance companies, investment managers, suppliers and government regulators all can contribute to the awareness of irregularities or deficiencies in the entity's operations. Careful record keeping, allocation of responsibility and reporting of actions become assets in resolving problems in the system.

(c) *Organization:* Structure and supervisory activities provide oversight of control functions and identification of deficiencies. Clerical duties control transaction processing, division of duties serves as a check on activities reducing fraud or errors.

(d) *Inventory Checking:* Data recorded by information systems is periodically checked against the physical assets and compared with accounting records.

(e) *Auditing:* A dedicated and competent internal and external auditing team will regularly provide recommendations and evaluations of the Internal Control system and its effectiveness.

(f) *Meetings:* Training seminars, planning sessions and other meetings provide valuable feedback on the effectiveness of controls and of personnel attitudes towards them.

(g) *Direct communication:* Personnel are asked periodically to state explicitly that they understand and comply with the code of ethics, policies and procedures and the Internal Control procedures. The statements can be verified by management or the audit committee.

Separate Evaluations

To supplement the ongoing monitoring activities it is useful to perform specific separate evaluations from time to time to assess the effectiveness of the system and the monitoring procedures.

(a) *Scope and Frequency:* The scope of the evaluation will depend on the objectives' categories – operations, financial reporting, and compliance – that are to be addressed, and the importance in terms of risk and impact on the organization, of the activity being evaluated. The frequency will be a function of the significance of the risks being controlled and the speed at which circumstances change.

(b) *Who Evaluates:* On a regular basis, self-assessments by frontline personnel, various levels of department heads and managers will feed the evaluation data upstream to the senior management executives who will consolidate and evaluate the information. The audit committee will perform internal control evaluations as part of their normal duties. From time to time external auditors may be called in for specific reasons or to get a fresh approach to the system and its effectiveness.

(c) *The Evaluation Process:* It is important that the evaluator understand completely the activity being evaluated and how it integrates with the greater picture, how and why the control system is applicable, and how each of the three categories are involved (operations, financial reporting and compliance). The process is useful in clarifying how a person's job fits into the whole process and how it is important to the success of the entity.

(d) *Methodology:* A wide variety of evaluation methodologies is available including checklists, questionnaires and flowcharts. Control objectives have been identified which will be applied and defined at each level of operations. Peer reviews and benchmarking against competitors can be useful.

(e) *Documentation:* While documentation is not always necessary to define operations and controls, it is easier to evaluate and test when job descriptions, operating instructions and information flow charts are available, particularly for external auditors. Too tight or restrictive rules and instructions can stifle innovation or individual initiative, so it is a value judgment that must be made to balance job performance with control effectiveness.

Action Plan

Following is a suggested outline for conducting evaluations of internal control systems.

(a) Decide on the scope of the evaluation.
(b) Identify applicable ongoing monitoring activities.
(c) Analyze evaluation work by internal and external auditors.
(d) Prioritize risk areas.
(e) Develop the evaluation program with short and long range segments.
(f) Assemble the parties to perform the evaluation.
(g) Discuss and agree on methodology, scope, tools, reports and documentation.

(h) Monitor progress and review findings.

(i) Ensure follow-up actions are taken, and integrate results into future evaluation segments.

Reporting Deficiencies

Deficiencies surface from time to time from a variety of sources. A deficiency is defined as a condition within an internal control system worthy of attention.

(a) *Sources of information:* Ongoing monitoring activities, internal and external evaluations all may uncover or identify deficiencies. External sources such as customers, vendors, government regulators and public accountants are also potential identifiers, either directly through perceiving a control problem or by identifying an operational or financial situation that leads back to a control deficiency.

(b) *What should be reported:* Obviously some things are of greater significance than others, and items reflecting a high degree of risk should be flagged for attention by management. Some parameters for reporting are:

(1) Any deficiency that can affect the entity's ability to attain its objectives **must** be reported.

(2) Any deficiency that indicates an ongoing or deeper problem may exist.

(3) Any deficiency that occurs because the activity was not covered by the internal control system.

(4) Any deficiency that might be insignificant on a one-time basis but could be serious if often repeated.

(c) *To whom to report:* Normally deficiencies would be reported by an individual to their immediate superior, and also to the person responsible for the function or activity involved. In this way notification of a problem will find its way upstream until it reaches the individual who is in a position to take corrective action, and to communicate to others in the organization that a situation exists which may affect their activities. Provision is also made for individuals to report sensitive information such as illegal or improper acts to higher management (including the audit committee) without fear of reprisal.

(d) *Reporting directives:* Protocols must be created at every level in an organization so that people are aware of the elements and activities that need to be reported and to whom. A documented paper trail should be incorporated so that follow-up and accountability may be addressed.

Limitations of Internal Control

Internal control, no matter how well designed and operated, can provide only reasonable assurance to management and the board of directors regarding achievement of an entity's objectives. The likelihood of achievement is affected by limitations inherent in all internal control systems. These include the realities that human judgment in decision making can be faulty, and that breakdowns can occur because of such human failures as simple error or mistake. Additionally, controls can be circumvented by the collusion of two or more people, and management has the ability to override the internal control system. Another limiting factor is the need to consider controls' relative costs and benefits.(COSO)

Some of the factors possibly limiting the effectiveness of internal control systems are:

(a) *Judgment:* Inexperience, pressure, lack of information, unrealistic objectives.
(b) *Breakdowns:* Misunderstanding instructions or objectives, carelessness, fatigue, distractions, forgetfulness or inadequate training.
(c) *Management Override:* (for illegitimate purposes) misrepresenting achievement levels, enhancing reported earnings, boosting market value, hiding lack of compliance.
(d) *Collusion:* Deliberate concealment, circumvention, data falsification.
(e) *Costs versus Benefits:* Measurement of cost/benefit ratios.

Roles and Responsibilities

Everyone in an organization has some responsibility for internal control. Management, however, is responsible for an entity's internal control system. The chief executive is ultimately responsible and should assume "ownership" of the control system. Financial and accounting officers are central to the way management exercises control, though all management personnel employ important roles and are accountable for controlling their units' activities. Similarly, internal auditors contribute to the ongoing effectiveness of the internal control system, but they do not have primary responsibility for establishing or maintaining it. The board of directors and its audit committee provide important oversight to the internal control system. A number of external parties, such as external auditors, often contribute to the achievement of an entity's objectives and provide information useful in effecting internal control. However, they are not responsible for the effectiveness of, nor are they a part of, the entity's internal control system.(COSO)

The roles of the various parties involved in the internal control system are:

(a) *Management:* CEO has ultimate responsibility, attitude, tone, influence, integrity and ethical values. Senior managers in charge of organizational units are responsible for controls within their units. Assign specific control functions and procedures to department heads and individual personnel.

(b) *Financial Officers:* CFO tracks and monitors performance in operations, finance and compliance. He/she is aware of all aspects of an entity's functioning. Prepares budgets and plans and is responsible for financial reporting. CFO is a key player in the organization.

(c) *Board of Directors:* Governance, guidance and oversight. High level objective setting and strategic planning. Directors are objective, capable and inquisitive. Oversight of internal control system.

(d) *Audit Committee:* Should be composed of independent directors. Provides oversight of activities, internal control system and financial reporting.

(e) *Internal Auditor(s):* Directly examine internal controls and recommend improvements; and,
  (1) Review the reliability and integrity of financial and operating information and the means used to identify, measure, classify and report such information;
  (2) Review the systems established to ensure compliance with those policies, plans, procedures, laws and regulations which could have a significant impact on operations and reports and should determine whether the organization is in compliance;
  (3) Review the means of safeguarding assets and, as appropriate, verify the existence of such assets;

(4) Appraise the economy and efficiency with which resources are employed;

(5) Review operations or programs to ascertain whether results are consistent with established objectives and goals and whether the operations or programs are being carried out as planned.

(f) *Other Personnel:* Internal control is everyone's responsibility; institute checks and balances; apply segregation of duties.

(g) *Effecting Control:* Reports, records, inspections, performance monitoring.

(h) *Reporting Problems:* Non-compliance, operating problems, illegal actions, safe methods of reporting.

(i) *External Auditors:* CPAs provide objective and independent views and analysis. They should not only report on financial statement presentation, but also on internal control effectiveness and compliance.

Summary

It is evident that establishing an Internal Control System that will satisfy the men and women in dark suits from the government is a time-consuming, expensive and complex project that will tax the resources of the company. Fortunately, the complexity and cost tend to be in proportion to the size of the organization, so the costs should reflect the ability to bear them. Most companies will have some systems in place already that can be adapted where necessary to satisfy requirements, but some integration and enhancement will probably be necessary, particularly in the auditing, assessment and monitoring areas.

Internal Control can be viewed as a Project Management exercise, where each "element" or "process" is considered as a specific "project." The same process used to manage a project can be used to manage these elements and processes, although generally in a simpler manner.

A careful evaluation of available software solutions is necessary, both to ensure that they actually will do the job, and also to determine how the selected system will integrate with existing systems in use in the company. Because of the expense and time involved in setting up the Internal Control system, serious research needs to be performed before embarking on a solution.

Appendix E provides a partial list of companies providing SOX solutions, and Appendix F provides a more detailed profile of one of them. The following charts will give you an idea of the scope of the exercise.

Typical Internal Control Data Flow Chart

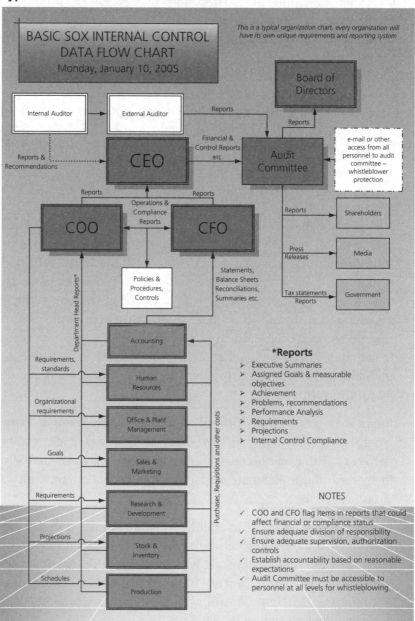

BASIC SOX INTERNAL CONTROL DATA FLOW CHART
Monday, January 10, 2005

This is a typical organization chart, every organization will have its own unique requirements and reporting system

Board of Directors

Internal Auditor

External Auditor — Reports

Reports

e-mail or other access from all personnel to audit committee – whistleblower protection

Reports & Recommendations

CEO

Financial & Control Reports etc.

Audit Committee

Reports

Reports

Operations & Compliance Reports

Reports — Shareholders

COO

CFO

Press Releases — Media

Department Head Reports*

Policies & Procedures, Controls

Statements, Balance Sheets Reconciliations, Summaries etc.

Tax statements Reports — Government

Accounting

*Reports
➢ Executive Summaries
➢ Assigned Goals & measurable objectives
➢ Achievement
➢ Problems, recommendations
➢ Performance Analysis
➢ Requirements
➢ Projections
➢ Internal Control Compliance

Requirements, standards

Human Resources

Organizational requirements

Office & Plant Management

Goals

Sales & Marketing

Purchases, Requisitions and other costs

Requirements

Research & Development

NOTES
✓ COO and CFO flag items in reports that could affect financial or compliance status
✓ Ensure adequate division of responsibility
✓ Ensure adequate supervision, authorization controls
✓ Establish accountability based on reasonable expectations
✓ Audit Committee must be accessible to personnel at all levels for whistleblowing.

Projections

Stock & Inventory

Schedules

Production

Internal Control System Chart

The Company

General Objective(s) – Mission Statement – To be loved by everyone, and to make the best widgets in the world.

Measurable Objective(s) – Make the Fortune 500 in 2007.
Risks – Poor Sales, High Overhead, inadequate personnel.
Controls – Hire qualified people, reduce waste, recycle, advertise.
Evaluation & Assessment – Were objectives met? Did controls work?
Owners: CEO, CFO, Senior Management, Board.

Business unit
(Sales, Accounting, R & D, Marketing, Warehouse & Inventory, Manufacturing, Engineering & Design, Shipping, etc.

General Objective(s) – Keep Customers happy, keep staff happy.
Objective(s) – Deliver on time, $100,000,00 in sales.
Risks – No product available, bad pricing, raw material shortage, strikes.
Controls – maintain inventories, look ahead, watch competition, anticipate.
Evaluation & Assessment – Were objectives met? Did controls work?
Owners: Vice presidents, Senior Management.

Process
Stock Control, Floor Sales, Debt Collection, Payroll, Media Relations, Fleet Maintenance, New Products

General Objective(s) – Keep buildings & grounds clean, keep noise down.
Measurable Objective(s) – Balance books, fleet 85% operational, 2 new products on market, In store sales $10,000,000.
Risks – Robberies, bad pricing, competitor advantage, computer malfunction, CFO runs off with stock clerk.
Controls – Building security, Back-up files, watch competition, anticipate.
Evaluation & Assessment – Were objectives met? Did controls work?
Owners: Department Heads, Middle Management.

Sub-Process
Packaging, Shelf stocking, Labeling, Banking, Salesmen, Drivers

General Objective(s) – Do my job well, pass along ideas.
Measurable Objective(s) – Maintain stock @ 300% monthly sales, $1,000,000 in sales per salesman, deliver within 10 days of order.
Risk – Illness, incompetence, discontentment, collusion.
Controls – mental & physical environment, training, bonuses, checks & balances, authorizations, access controls.
Evaluation & Assessment –Were objectives met? Did control work?
Owner: Supervisors, Staff.

The Internal Control System

Information Technology Department (IT)

Develops, Integrates and maintains the software solution(s) to acquire Information, dispense information, collect and organize data, provide assessment and audit systems, and generate reports at each level.

Appendix A—Final Rules

Summary of the final rules

The final rules require the annual report of every company that files periodic reports under section 13(a) or 15(d) of the Exchange Act, other than reports by registered investment companies, to contain a report of management that includes:

A statement of management's responsibility for establishing and maintaining adequate internal control over financial reporting for the company;

A statement identifying the framework used by management to evaluate the effectiveness of the company's internal control over financial reporting;

Management's assessment of the effectiveness of the company's internal control over financial reporting, as of the end of the most recent fiscal year; and

A statement that the registered public accounting firm that audited the financial statements included in the annual report has issued an attestation report on management's evaluation of the company's internal control over financial reporting.

We are adding these requirements pursuant to the legislative mandate in section 404 of the Sarbanes–Oxley Act. Under our final rules, a company also will be required to evaluate and disclose any change in its internal control over financial reporting that occurred during the fiscal quarter that has materially affected, or is reasonably likely to materially affect, the company's internal control over financial reporting.

We are also adopting amendments to require companies to file the certifications mandated by sections 302 and 906 of the Sarbanes–Oxley Act as exhibits to their annual, semi-annual and quarterly reports. These amendments will enhance the ability of investors, the Commission staff, the Department of Justice and other interested parties to easily and efficiently access the certifications through our Electronic Data Gathering, Analysis and Retrieval ("EDGAR") system and facilitate better monitoring of a company's compliance with the certification requirements.

Certification Form*

[Signature]   I, [identify the certifying individual], certify that:

I have reviewed this [specify report] of [identify small business issuer];

Based on my knowledge, this report does not contain any untrue statement of a material fact or omit to state a material fact necessary to make the statements made, in light of the circumstances under which such statements were made, nor misleading with respect to the period covered by this report;

Based on my knowledge, the financial statements, and other financial information included in this report, fairly present in all material respects the financial condition, results of operations and cash flows of the small business issuer as of, and for, the periods presented in this report;

The small business issuer's other certifying officer(s) and I are responsible for establishing and maintaining disclosure controls and procedures (as defined in Exchange Act Rules 13a-15(e) and 15d-15(e)) and internal control over financial reporting (as defined in Exchange Act Rules 13a-15(f) and 15d-15(f)) for the small business issuer and have:

(a) Designed such disclosure controls and procedures, or caused such disclosure controls and procedures to be designed under our supervision, to ensure that material information relating to the small business issuer, including its consolidated subsidiaries, is made known to us by others within those entities, particularly during the period in which this report is being prepared;

(b) Designed such internal control over financial reporting, or caused such internal control over financial reporting to be designed under our supervision, to provide reasonable assurance regarding the reliability of financial reporting and the preparation of financial statements for external purposes in accordance with generally accepted accounting principles;

(c) Evaluated the effectiveness of the small business issuer's disclosure controls and procedures and presented in this report our conclusions about the effectiveness of the disclosure controls and procedures, as of the end of the period covered by this report based on such evaluation; and

---

* Provide a separate certification for each principal executive officer and principal financial officer of the small business issuer. See Rules 13a-14(a) and 15d-14(a).

(d) Disclosed in this report any change in the small business issuer's internal control over financial reporting that occurred during the small business issuer's most recent fiscal quarter (the small business issuer's fourth fiscal quarter in the case of an annual report) that has materially affected, or is reasonably likely to materially affect, the small business issuer's internal control over financial reporting; and,

The small business issuer's other certifying officer(s) and I have disclosed, based on our most recent evaluation of internal control over financial reporting, to the small business issuer's auditors and the audit committee of the small business issuer's board of directors (or persons performing the equivalent functions):

(a) All significant deficiencies and material weaknesses in the design or operation of internal control over financial reporting which are reasonably likely to adversely affect the small business issuer's ability to record, process, summarize and report financial information; and

(b) Any fraud, whether or not material, that involves management or other employees who have a significant role in the small business issuer's internal control over financial reporting.

Date: ——

_____

[Name]

_____

[Title]

Provide the certifications required by Rule 13a-14(b) (17 CFR 240.13a-14(b)) or Rule 15d-14(b) (17 CFR 240.15d-14(b)) and section 1350 of Chapter 63 of Title 18 of the United States Code (18 U.S.C. 1350) as an exhibit to this report.

A certification furnished pursuant to Rule 13a-14(b) (17 CFR 240.13a-14(b)) or Rule 15d-14(b) (17 CFR 240.15d-14(b)) and section 1350 of Chapter 63 of Title 18 of the United States Code (18 U.S.C. 1350) will not be deemed "filed" for purposes of Section 18 of the Exchange Act [15 U.S.C. 78r], or otherwise subject to the liability of that section. Such certification will not be deemed to be incorporated by reference into any filing under the Securities Act or the Exchange Act, except to the extent that the issuer specifically incorporates it by reference.

Disclosure controls and procedures   Where the Form is being used as an annual report filed under section 13(a) or 15(d) of the Exchange Act, disclose the conclusions of the issuer's principal executive and principal financial officers, or persons performing similar functions, regarding the effectiveness of the issuer's disclosure controls and procedures (as defined in 17 CFR 240.13a-15(e) or 240.15d-15(e)) as of the end of the period covered by the report, based on the evaluation of these controls and procedures required by paragraph (b) of 17 CFR 240.13a-15 or 240.15d-15.

Management's annual report on internal control over financial reporting   Where the Form is being used as an annual report filed under section 13(a) or 15(d) of the Exchange Act, provide a report of management on the issuer's internal control over financial reporting (as defined in 17 CFR 240.13a-15(f) or 240.15d-15(f)) that contains:

(1) A statement of management's responsibility for establishing and maintaining adequate internal control over financial reporting for the issuer;

(2) A statement identifying the framework used by management to evaluate the effectiveness of the issuer's internal control over financial reporting as required by paragraph (c) of 17 CFR 240.13a-15 or 240.15d-15;

(3) Management's assessment of the effectiveness of the issuer's internal control over financial reporting as of the end of the issuer's most recent fiscal year, including a statement as to whether or not internal control over financial reporting is effective. This discussion must include disclosure of any material weakness in the issuer's internal control over financial reporting identified by management. Management is not permitted to conclude that the issuer's internal control over financial reporting is effective if there are one or more material weaknesses in the issuer's internal control over financial reporting; and

(4) A statement that the registered public accounting firm that audited the financial statements included in the annual report containing the disclosure required by this Item has issued an attestation report on management's assessment of the issuer's internal control over financial reporting.

Attestation report of the registered public accounting firm   Where the Form is being used as an annual report filed under Section

13(a) or 15(d) of the Exchange Act, provide the registered public accounting firm's attestation report on management's assessment of internal control over financial reporting in the annual report containing the disclosure required by this Item.

Changes in internal control over financial reporting Disclose any change in the issuer's internal control over financial reporting identified in connection with the evaluation required by paragraph (d) of 17 CFR 240.13a-15 or 240.15d-15 that occurred during the period covered by the annual report that has materially affected, or is reasonably likely to materially affect, the issuer's internal control over financial reporting.

Instructions to paragraphs (b), (c), (d) and (e) of General Instruction B. 6.

(1) The issuer must maintain evidential matter, including documentation, to provide reasonable support for management's assessment of the effectiveness of the issuer's internal control over financial reporting.

(2) An issuer that is an Asset-Backed Issuer (as defined in 17 CFR 240.13a-14(g) and 240.15d-14(g)) is not required to disclose the information required by this Item.

Definition of internal control

1. Proposed rule

The proposed rules would have defined the term "internal controls and procedures for financial reporting" to mean controls that pertain to the preparation of financial statements for external purposes that are fairly presented in conformity with generally accepted accounting principles as addressed by the Codification of Statements on Auditing Standards §319 or any superseding definition or other literature that is issued or adopted by the Public Company Accounting Oversight Board.

As noted in the Proposing Release, there has been some confusion over the exact meaning and scope of the term "internal control," because the definition of the term has evolved over time. Historically, the term "internal control" was applied almost exclusively within the accounting profession. As the auditing of financial statements evolved from a process of detailed testing of transactions and account balances towards a process of sampling and testing, greater consideration of a company's internal controls became necessary in planning an audit. If an internal control component had been adequately designed, then the auditor could limit further consideration of that control to procedures to determine whether the control had been placed in operation. Accordingly, the auditor could rely on the control to serve as a basis to reduce the amount, timing or extent of substantive testing in the execution of an audit. Conversely, if an auditor determined that an internal control component was inadequate in its design or operation, then the auditor could not rely upon that control. In this instance, the auditor would conduct tests of transactions and perform additional analyses in order to accumulate sufficient, competent audit evidence to support its opinion on the financial statements.

From the outset, it was recognized that internal control is a broad concept that extends beyond the accounting functions of a company. Early attempts to define the term focused primarily on clarifying the portion of a company's internal control that an auditor should consider when planning and performing an audit of a company's financial statements. However, this did not improve the level of understanding of the term, nor satisfactorily provide the guidance sought by auditors. Successive definitions and formal studies of the concept of internal control followed.

In 1977, based on recommendations of the Commission, Congress enacted the Foreign Corrupt Practices Act (FCPA). The FCPA codified the accounting control provisions contained in Statement of Auditing Standards No. 1 (codified as AU §320 in the Codification of Statements on Auditing Standards). Under the FCPA, companies that have a class of securities registered under section 12 of the Exchange Act, or that are required to file reports under section 15(d) of the Exchange Act, are required to devise and maintain a system of internal accounting controls sufficient to provide reasonable assurances that:

(a) transactions are executed in accordance with management's general or specific authorization;
(b) transactions are recorded as necessary (1) to permit preparation of financial statements in conformity with generally accepted accounting principles or any other criteria applica-

ble to such statements, and (2) to maintain accountability for assets;

(c) access to assets is permitted only in accordance with management's general or specific authorization; and

(d) the recorded accountability for assets is compared with the existing assets at reasonable intervals and appropriate action is taken with respect to any differences.

In 1985, a private-sector initiative known as the National Commission on Fraudulent Financial Reporting, also known as the Treadway Commission, was formed to study the financial reporting system in the United States. In 1987, the Treadway Commission issued a report recommending that its sponsoring organizations work together to integrate the various internal control concepts and definitions and to develop a common reference point.

In response, the Committee of Sponsoring Organizations of the Treadway Commission (COSO) undertook an extensive study of internal control to establish a common definition that would serve the needs of companies, independent public accountants, legislators and regulatory agencies, and to provide a broad framework of criteria against which companies could evaluate the effectiveness of their internal control systems. In 1992, COSO published its Internal Control—Integrated Framework. The COSO Framework defined internal control as "a process, effected by an entity's board of directors, management and other personnel, designed to provide reasonable assurance regarding the achievement of objectives" in three categories—effectiveness and efficiency of operations; reliability of financial reporting; and compliance with applicable laws and regulations. COSO further stated that internal control consists of: the control environment, risk assessment, control activities, information and communication, and monitoring. The scope of internal control therefore extends to policies, plans, procedures, processes, systems, activities, functions, projects, initiatives, and endeavors of all types at all levels of a company.

In 1995, the AICPA incorporated the definition of internal control set forth in the COSO Report in Statement on Auditing Standards No. 78 (codified as AU §319 in the Codification of Statements on Auditing Standards). Although we recognized that the AU §319 definition was derived from the COSO definition, our proposal referred to AU §319 because we thought that the former constituted a more formal and widely accessible version of the definition than the latter.

2. Comments on the proposal

We received comments from 25 commentators on the proposed definition of "internal control and procedures for financial reporting." Eleven commentators stated that the proposed definition of internal control was appropriate or generally agreed with the proposal. Two of these noted that the definition in AU §319 had been adopted by the bank regulatory agencies for use by banking institutions. Fourteen of the 25 commentators opposed the proposed definition. Two of these asserted that the proposed definition was too complex and would not resolve the confusion that existed over the meaning or scope of the term.

Several of the commentators that were opposed to the proposed definition thought that we should refer to COSO for the definition of internal control, rather than AU §319. Some of these commentators noted that the objective of AU §319 is to provide guidance to auditors regarding their consideration of internal control in planning and performing an audit of financial statements. The common concern of these commentators was that AU §319 does not provide any measure or standard by which a company's management can determine that internal control is effective, nor does it define what constitutes effective internal control. One commenter believed that absent such evaluative criteria or definition of effectiveness, the proposed rules could not be implemented effectively. In addition, several of the commentators opposed to the proposed definition suggested that we use the term "internal control over financial reporting" rather than the term "internal controls and procedures for financial reporting," on the ground that the former is more consistent with the terminology currently used within the auditing literature.

A few of the commentators urged us to adopt a considerably broader definition of internal control that would focus not only on internal control over financial reporting, but also on internal control objectives associated with enterprise risk management and corporate governance. While we agree that these are important objectives, the definition that we are adopting retains a focus on financial reporting, consistent with our position articulated in the Proposing Release. We are not adopting a more expansive definition of internal control for a variety of reasons. Most important, we believe that section 404 focuses on the element of internal control that relates to financial reporting. In addition, many commentators indicated that even the more limited definition related to financial reporting that we proposed will impose substantial reporting and cost burdens on companies. Finally, independent accountants traditionally have not been responsible for reviewing and testing, or attesting to an assessment by management of, internal controls that are outside the boundary of financial reporting.

3. Final rules

After consideration of the comments, we have decided to make several modifications to the proposed amendments. We agree that we should use the term "internal control over financial reporting" in our amendments to implement section 404, as well as our revisions to the section 302 certification requirements and forms of certification. Rapidly changing terminology has been one obstacle in the development of an accepted understanding of internal control. The term "internal control over financial reporting" is the predominant term used by companies and auditors and best encompasses the objectives of the Sarbanes–Oxley Act. In addition, by using this term, we avoid having to familiarize investors, companies and auditors with new terminology, which should lessen any confusion that may exist about the meaning and scope of internal control.

The final rules define "internal control over financial reporting" as:

A process designed by, or under the supervision of, the registrant's principal executive and principal financial officers, or persons performing similar functions, and effected by the registrant's board of directors, management and other personnel, to provide reasonable assurance regarding the reliability of financial reporting and the preparation of financial statements for external purposes in accordance with generally accepted accounting principles and includes those policies and procedures that:

(1) Pertain to the maintenance of records that in reasonable detail accurately and fairly reflect the transactions and dispositions of the assets of the registrant;
(2) Provide reasonable assurance that transactions are recorded as necessary to permit preparation of financial statements in accordance with generally accepted accounting principles, and that

receipts and expenditures of the registrant are being made only in accordance with authorizations of management and directors of the registrant; and

(3) Provide reasonable assurance regarding prevention or timely detection of unauthorized acquisition, use or disposition of the registrant's assets that could have a material effect on the financial statements.

We recognize that our definition of the term "internal control over financial reporting" reflected in the final rules encompasses the subset of internal controls addressed in the COSO Report that pertains to financial reporting objectives. Our definition does not encompass the elements of the COSO Report definition that relate to effectiveness and efficiency of a company's operations and a company's compliance with applicable laws and regulations, with the exception of compliance with the applicable laws and regulations directly related to the preparation of financial statements, such as the Commission's financial reporting requirements. Our definition is consistent with the description of internal accounting controls in Exchange Act Section 13(b)(2)(B).

Following the general language defining internal control over financial reporting, clauses (1) and (2) include the internal control matters described in section 103 of the Sarbanes–Oxley Act that the company's registered public accounting firm is required to evaluate in its audit or attestation report. This language is included to make clear that the assessment of management in its internal control report as to which the company's registered public accounting firm will be required to attest and report specifically covers the matters referenced in section 103. A few commentators believed that it would cause confusion if the definition of internal control did not acknowledge the objectives set forth in section 103 of the Sarbanes–Oxley Act. As discussed in section II.G below, the PCAOB is responsible for establishing the section 103 standards.

Our definition also includes, in clause (3), explicit reference to assurances regarding use or disposition of the company's assets. This provision is specifically included to make clear that, for purposes of our definition, the safeguarding of assets is one of the elements of internal control over financial reporting and it addresses the supplementation of the COSO Framework after it was originally promulgated. In the absence of our change to the definition, the determination of whether control regarding the safeguarding of assets falls within a company's internal control over financial reporting currently could be subject to varying interpretation.

Safeguarding of assets had been a primary objective of internal accounting control in SAS No. 1. In 1988, the ASB issued Statement of Auditing Standards No. 55 (codified as AU §319 in the Codification of Statements on Auditing Standards), which replaced AU §320. SAS No. 55 revised the definition of "internal control" and expanded auditors' responsibilities for considering internal control in a financial statement audit. The prior classification of internal control into the two categories of "internal accounting control" and "administrative control" was replaced with the single term "internal control structure," which consisted of three interrelated components—control environment, the accounting system and control procedures. Under this new definition, the safeguarding of assets was no longer a primary objective, but a subset of the control procedures component. The COSO Report followed this shift in the iteration of safeguarding of assets. The COSO Report states that operations objectives "pertain to effectiveness and efficiency of the entity's operations, including performance and profitability goals and safeguarding resources against loss." However, the report also clarifies that safeguarding of assets can fall within other categories of internal control.

In 1994, COSO published an addendum to the Reporting to External Parties volume of the COSO Report. The addendum was issued in response to a concern expressed by some parties, including the U.S. General Accounting Office, that the management reports contemplated by the COSO Report did not adequately address controls relating to safeguarding of assets and therefore would not fully respond to the requirements of the FCPA. In the addendum, COSO concluded that while it believed its definition of internal control in its 1992 report remained appropriate, it recognized that the FCPA encompasses certain controls related to safeguarding of assets and that there is a reasonable expectation on the part of some readers of management's internal control reports that the reports will cover such controls. The addendum therefore sets forth the following definition of the term "internal control over safeguarding of assets against unauthorized acquisition, use or disposition":

Internal control over safeguarding of assets against unauthorized acquisition, use or disposition is a process, effected by an entity's board of directors, management and other personnel, designed to provide reasonable assurance regarding prevention or timely detection of unauthorized acquisition, use or disposition of the entity's assets that could have a material effect on the financial statements.

As indicated above, to achieve the desired result and to provide consistency with COSO's 1994 addendum, we have incorporated this definition into our definition of "internal control over financial reporting." We are persuaded that this is appropriate given the fact that our definition will be used for purposes of public management reporting, and that the companies that will be subject to the section 404 requirements also are subject to the FCPA requirements. So, under the final rules, safeguarding of assets as provided is specifically included in our definition of "internal control over financial reporting."

Appendix B—SE Act 10A

Securities Exchange Act of 1934: Section l0A—Audit requirements

In general

Each audit required pursuant to this title of the financial statements of an issuer by a registered public accounting firm shall include, in accordance with generally accepted auditing standards, as may be modified or supplemented from time to time by the Commission—

(a) procedures designed to provide reasonable assurance of detecting illegal acts that would have a direct and material effect on the determination of financial statement amounts;
(b) procedures designed to identify related party transactions that are material to the financial statements or otherwise require disclosure therein; and
(c) an evaluation of whether there is substantial doubt about the ability of the issuer to continue as a going concern during the ensuing fiscal year.
(d) Required response to audit discoveries.

Investigation and report to management

If, in the course of conducting an audit pursuant to this title to which subsection (a) of this section applies, the registered public accounting firm detects or otherwise becomes aware of information indicating that an illegal act (whether or not perceived to have a material effect on the financial statements of the issuer) has or may have occurred, the firm shall, in accordance with generally accepted auditing standards, as may be modified or supplemented from time to time by the Commission—

(a) determine whether it is likely that an illegal act has occurred; and
(b) if so, determine and consider the possible effect of the illegal act on the financial statements of the issuer, including any contingent monetary effects, such as fines, penalties and damages; and

as soon as practicable, inform the appropriate level of the management of the issuer and assure that the audit committee of the issuer, or the board of directors of the issuer in the absence of such a committee, is adequately informed with respect to illegal acts that have been detected or have otherwise come to the attention of such firm in the course of the audit, unless the illegal act is clearly inconsequential.

Response to failure to take remedial action

If, after determining that the audit committee of the board of directors of the issuer, or the board of directors of the issuer in the absence of an audit committee, is adequately informed with respect to illegal acts that have been detected or have otherwise come to the attention of the firm in the course of the audit of such firm, the registered public accounting firm concludes that—

(a) the illegal act has a material effect on the financial statements of the issuer;

(b) the senior management has not taken, and the board of directors has not caused senior management to take, timely and appropriate remedial actions with respect to the illegal act; and

(c) the failure to take remedial action is reasonably expected to warrant departure from a standard report of the auditor, when made, or warrant resignation from the audit engagement;

the registered public accounting firm shall, as soon as practicable, directly report its conclusions to the board of directors.

Notice to Commission; response to failure to notify

An issuer whose board of directors receives a report under paragraph (2) shall inform the Commission by notice not later than one business day after the receipt of such report and shall furnish the registered public accounting firm making such report with a copy of the notice furnished to the Commission. If the registered public accounting firm fails to receive a copy of the notice before the expiration of the required 1-business-day period, the registered public accounting firm shall—

(a) resign from the engagement; or

(b) furnish to the Commission a copy of its report (or the documentation of any oral report given) not later than one business day following such failure to receive notice.

Report after resignation

If a registered public accounting firm resigns from an engagement under paragraph (3)(A), the firm shall, not later than one business day following the failure by the issuer to notify the Commission under paragraph (3), furnish to the Commission a copy of the report of the firm (or the documentation of any oral report given).

Auditor liability limitation

No registered public accounting firm shall be liable in a private action for any finding, conclusion, or statement expressed in a report made pursuant to paragraph (3) or (4) of subsection (b) of this section, including any rule promulgated pursuant thereto.

Civil penalties in cease-and-desist proceedings

If the Commission finds, after notice and opportunity for hearing in a proceeding instituted pursuant to section 21C, that a registered public accounting firm has willfully violated paragraph (3) or (4) of subsection (b) of this section, the Commission may, in addition to entering an order under section 21C, impose a civil penalty against the registered public accounting firm and any other person that the Commission finds was a cause of such violation. The determination to impose a civil penalty and the amount of the penalty shall be governed by the standards set forth in section 21B.

Preservation of existing authority

Except as provided in subsection (d) of this section, nothing in this section shall be held to limit or otherwise affect the authority of the Commission under this title.

Definitions

As used in this section, the term "illegal act" means an act or omission that violates any law, or any rule or regulation having the force of law. As used in this section, the term "issuer" means an issuer (as defined in section 3), the securities of which are registered under section 12, or that is required to file reports pursuant to section 15(d), or that files or has filed a registration statement that has not yet become effective under the Securities Act of 1933, and that it has not withdrawn.

Prohibited activities

Except as provided in subsection (h), it shall be unlawful for a registered public accounting firm (and any associated person of that firm, to the extent determined appropriate by the Commission) that performs for any issuer any audit required by this title or the rules of the Commission under this title or, beginning 180 days after the date of commencement of the operations of the Public Company Accounting Oversight Board established under section 101 of the Sarbanes–Oxley Act of 2002 (in this section referred to as the "Board"), the rules of the Board, to provide to that issuer, contemporaneously with the audit, any non-audit service, including—

(a) bookkeeping or other services related to the accounting records or financial statements of the audit client;
(b) financial information systems design and implementation;
(c) appraisal or valuation services, fairness opinions, or contribution-in-kind reports;
(d) actuarial services;
(e) internal audit outsourcing services;
(f) management functions or human resources;
(g) broker or dealer, investment adviser, or investment banking services;
(h) legal services and expert services unrelated to the audit; and
(i) any other service that the Board determines, by regulation, is impermissible.

Pre-approval required for non-audit services

A registered public accounting firm may engage in any non-audit service, including tax services, that is not described in any of paragraphs (1) through (9) of subsection (g) for an audit client, only if the activity is approved in advance by the audit committee of the issuer, in accordance with subsection (i).

Pre-approval requirements

In general

Audit committee action

All auditing services (which may entail providing comfort letters in connection with securities underwritings or statutory audits required for insurance companies for purposes of State law) and non-audit services, other than as provided in subparagraph (B), provided to an issuer by the auditor of the issuer shall be pre-approved by the audit committee of the issuer.

De minimus exception

The pre-approval requirement under subparagraph (A) is waived with respect to the provision of non-audit services for an issuer, if—

(a) the aggregate amount of all such non-audit services provided to the issuer constitutes not more than 5 percent of the total amount of revenues paid by the issuer to its auditor during the fiscal year in which the non-audit services are provided;

(b) such services were not recognized by the issuer at the time of the engagement to be non-audit services; and

(c) such services are promptly brought to the attention of the audit committee of the issuer and approved prior to the completion of the audit by the audit committee or by one or more members of the audit committee who are members of the board of directors to whom authority to grant such approvals has been delegated by the audit committee.

Disclosure to investors

Approval by an audit committee of an issuer under this subsection of a non-audit service to be performed by the auditor of the issuer shall be disclosed to investors in periodic reports required by section 13(a).

Delegation authority

The audit committee of an issuer may delegate to one or more designated members of the audit committee who are independent directors of the board of directors the authority to grant pre-approvals required by this subsection. The decisions of any member to whom authority is delegated under this paragraph to pre-approve an activity under this subsection shall be presented to the full audit committee at each of its scheduled meetings.

Approval of audit services for other purposes

In carrying out its duties under subsection (m)(2), if the audit committee of an issuer approves an audit service within the scope of the engagement of the auditor, such audit service shall be deemed to have been pre-approved for purposes of this subsection.

Audit partner rotation

It shall be unlawful for a registered public accounting firm to provide audit services to an issuer if the lead (or coordinating) audit partner (having primary responsibility for the audit), or the audit partner responsible for reviewing the audit, has performed audit services for that issuer in each of the five previous fiscal years of that issuer.

Reports to audit committees

Each registered public accounting firm that performs for any issuer any audit required by this title shall timely report to the audit committee of the issuer—

(a) all critical accounting policies and practices to be used;
(b) all alternative treatments of financial information within generally accepted accounting principles that have been discussed with management officials of the issuer, ramifications of the use of such alternative disclosures and treatments, and the treatment preferred by the registered public accounting firm; and
(c) other material written communications between the registered public accounting firm and the management of the issuer, such as any management letter or schedule of unadjusted differences.

Conflicts of interest

It shall be unlawful for a registered public accounting firm to perform for an issuer any audit service required by this title, if a chief executive officer, controller, chief financial officer, chief accounting officer, or any person serving in an equivalent position for the issuer, was employed by that registered independent public accounting firm and participated in any capacity in the audit of that issuer during the one-year period preceding the date of the initiation of the audit.

Standards relating to audit committees

Commission rules

In general

Effective not later than 270 days after the date of enactment of this subsection, the Commission shall, by rule, direct the national securities exchanges and national securities associations to prohibit the listing of any security of an issuer that is not in compliance with the requirements of any portion of paragraphs (2) through (6).

Opportunity to cure defects

The rules of the Commission under subparagraph (A) shall provide for appropriate procedures for an issuer to have an opportunity to cure any defects that would be the basis for a prohibition under subparagraph (A), before the imposition of such prohibition.

Responsibilities relating to registered public accounting firms

The audit committee of each issuer, in its capacity as a committee of the board of directors, shall be directly responsible for the appointment, compensation, and oversight of the work of any registered public accounting firm employed by that issuer (including resolution of disagreements between management and the auditor regarding financial reporting) for the purpose of preparing or issuing an audit report or related work, and each such registered public accounting firm shall report directly to the audit committee.

Independence

In general

Each member of the audit committee of the issuer shall be a member of the board of directors of the issuer, and shall otherwise be independent.

Criteria

In order to be considered to be independent for purposes of this paragraph, a member of an audit committee of an issuer may not, other than in his or her capacity as a member of the audit committee, the board of directors, or any other board committee—

(a) accept any consulting, advisory, or other compensatory fee from the issuer; or
(b) be an affiliated person of the issuer or any subsidiary thereof.

Exemption authority

The Commission may exempt from the requirements of subparagraph (B) a particular relationship with respect to audit committee members, as the Commission determines appropriate in light of the circumstances.

Complaints

Each audit committee shall establish procedures for—

(a) the receipt, retention, and treatment of complaints received by the issuer regarding accounting, internal accounting controls, or auditing matters; and
(b) the confidential, anonymous submission by employees of the issuer of concerns regarding questionable accounting or auditing matters.

Authority to engage advisers

Each audit committee shall have the authority to engage independent counsel and other advisers, as it determines necessary to carry out its duties.

Funding

Each issuer shall provide for appropriate funding, as determined by the audit committee, in its capacity as a committee of the board of directors, for payment of compensation—

(a) to the registered public accounting firm employed by the issuer for the purpose of rendering or issuing an audit report; and

(b) to any advisers employed by the audit committee under paragraph (5).

Appendix C—Compliance Review

What do I have to do?

Q. As the CEO, CFO, or COO, what steps should I take to get the process of implementing SOX compliance underway?

A. Here is a typical and reasonable approach to getting started.

(1) Call a Board meeting and
  (a) Decide whether to create an Audit Committee or have the Board take the responsibility. Decide on the committee members or Board members who will perform the tasks. Appoint an Internal Auditor.
  (b) Confirm that the company, its officers, directors, and management will behave in an ethical, trustworthy, and legal manner in the performance of their duties. This may seem obvious but few companies actually have it on record (minutes) that this is their intention.
  (c) Have at least the CFO and other financial officers read and signed the Code of Ethics. (Appendix D)
  (d) Appoint a Compliance Director (CD) who will oversee the compliance process and implement the Internal Control System. (Could be the Internal Auditor)
  (e) Discuss the scope and provide guidelines and then authorize a preliminary budget of compliance and Internal Control objectives.
  (f) Instruct the CD to prepare a plan with measurable objectives and budget requirements within a reasonable period, which will then be presented to the Board for approval and final budget approval.
(2) Initiate a Policies and Procedures Manual (or revive an existing one) and place someone in charge of bringing it in line with SOX compliance requirements. They will work hand in hand with the CD.
(3) Brief the entire company regarding SOX and its implications for the company and employees. Explain the necessity of compliance and everyone's role and importance. Prepare everyone for some distractions and interruptions during the implementation process and for some changes in their job descriptions and work habits during and after implementation.

A CDROM containing a PowerPoint Presentation aimed at company personnel is included with this book.

A Template for a letter to clients, suppliers, and associates informing them of the company's intention to become SOX compliant, and the possible implications to the client, supplier, or associate is included as Template 3.1.

(4) Run through the compliance review checklist (see below) and take care of all the smaller items (other than 302/404), then check them off.

(5) Provide high level support to the CD in the setting up and implementation of compliance requirements and the Internal Control System.

Checklist

Please refer to the appropriate section for details of the requirement.

Section	Action	Completed (Signed)
102	Obtain written confirmation	
103	Obtain written confirmation	
105	Obtain written confirmation	
106	Obtain written confirmation	
108	Obtain written confirmation	
201	Have Audit Committee check & confirm. Entry in P&P Manual	
202	Have Audit Committee check & confirm.	
203	Audit Committee keep records and monitor.	
204	Audit Committee retain written log and reports	
205	Establish an Audit Committee if not already formed.	
206	Check for conflict, remedy if necessary	
301	Audit Committee to fully understand requirements Sec. 10A Ensure full compliance. Entry in P&P Manual re. Audit Com responsibilities. Create complaint/concern procedures.	
302	Establish Internal Control System (see Chapter 2 for details) Use official certification format. (Appendix D) Describe System in P&P Manual	
303	Maintain a log and minutes of all meetings	
304	Retain a complete record of reimbursements if applicable.	

Section	Action	Completed (Signed)
306	Insert prohibition in P&P Manual	
401	Alert CFO & Acc. Dept of provisions of this section. Insert in P&P	
402	Alert CFO & Acc. Dept of provisions of this section. Insert in P&P	
403	Notify all 10% + shareholders. Insert rule & form in P&P Manual	
404	Confirm that 302 has been initiated and is effective Confirm Internal Control System is complete and operational.	
406	Create a code of ethics for all senior management & officers. All to sign. Describe in P&P Manual	
407	Audit Committee to ensure compliance	
409	Create a medium for ensuring info is disseminated to shareholders. Appoint an officer to ensure this is done regularly.	
501	Audit Committee to ensure no conflict of interest exists	
604	Audit Committee to ensure brokers/dealers are in compliance	
802	Clean up and refine filing and record system to comply Enter description and responsibilities in P&P Manual	
806	Create a system for employee reporting. Describe in P&P Manual	

807	Obtain legal counsel regarding any securities sales.	
906	See Sec. 302, ensure correct certification format is used	
1001	CEO must be aware of accuracy of the Tax Return Third party evaluation may be desirable.	
1102	Entry in P&P Manual regarding maintaining integrity of documents.	
1107	Entry in P&P Manual	

Corporate governance in Canada and the UK

While any Canadian or UK company which meets the conditions outlined in the "Definitions," Section 2 of the Sarbanes–Oxley Act as an "Issuer" or "Foreign Private Issuer" must comply with the SOX Act requirements or face possible action by the SEC, companies who are not required to comply with SOX still face regulatory action by the Canadian and UK governments.

The compliance requirements being imposed are not quite as onerous or punitive as the US solution, but they are still going to require significant and probably expensive resolution.

The UK legislation, the full name of which is The Companies (Audit, Investigations and Community Enterprise) Bill, will impose new measures upon UK firms to:

> ensure all data relating to trades, transactions and all accounting practices throughout the organisation are auditable.

The full text of the new bill is available at http:// www.legislation. hmso.gov.uk/acts/acts2004/20040027.htm

While the wording is different, the essence is similar. A system must be present within a company that will enable an external auditor to be able to fully understand and evaluate any company activities or situations that affect its financial well-being. In other words, transparency and accessibility. Further, auditors are expected to be independent and to clearly disclose any other work, functions, or services they perform for a client, and the directors and officers of the company are required to assert that the information they provide is both accurate and true.

Establishing an internal control system based on the concepts outlined in this book should enable a company to be in compliance with the UK Companies Bill.

In Canada, the new rules are close to the SOX rules. Once again, if the SOX rules are complied with, they should be more than adequate to ensure Canadian disclosure and control requirements.

The substance of the final rules to come into force on March 30, 2004 can be summarized as follows.

Certification: Multilateral Instrument 52–109

Similar to SOX, the first rule requires CEOs and CFOs of all Canadian public companies (including income trusts) to personally certify:

◆ that, to their knowledge, the issuer's *annual or interim filings*, as the case may be, *do not contain any misrepresentations or omissions* and that, together with the annual and interim financial statements, they *fairly present in all material respects the issuer's financial condition, results of operations and cash flows.* Annual and interim filings include an issuer's annual information form, annual and interim financial statements, and annual and interim MD&A.

◆ that they have designed such *disclosure controls and procedures* and such *internal control over financial reporting* (defined similarly to the SEC definitions) to provide reasonable assurance (i) that material information relating to the issuer is made known to them, and (ii) regarding the reliability of financial reporting and the preparation of financial statements for external purposes in accordance with generally accepted accounting principles (subject to transitional provisions).

◆ that they have evaluated the *effectiveness* of the issuer's disclosure controls and procedures and have caused the issuer to disclose in the annual MD&A their conclusions about the effectiveness of the disclosure controls and procedures (subject to transitional provisions).

◆ that they have caused the issuer to disclose in the annual MD&A or interim MD&A, as the case may be, any *change* in the internal control over financial reporting that occurred and has materially affected, or is reasonably likely to materially affect, the internal control over financial reporting (subject to transitional provisions).

Audit Committees: Multilateral Instrument 52–110

This rule will require that:

◆ audit committees have a minimum of three directors
◆ each member be independent, and
◆ each member be financially literate.

The definition of *independent* is closely parallel to the US definition and refers to the absence of any direct or indirect material relationship with the issuer. This includes a relationship that could, in the view of the board of directors, reasonably interfere with the exercise of a director's independent judgment. Certain prescribed relationships will cause a person to be deemed to have a material relationship with the issuer.

Financial literacy is defined as the ability to read and understand a set of financial statements that present a breadth and level of complexity of accounting issues that are generally comparable to the breadth and complexity of the issues that can reasonably be expected to be raised by the issuer's financial statements. Audit committee members who do not have, at the time of their appointment, the required financial literacy will be *permitted to become financially literate* within a reasonable period of time, subject to disclosure of such fact.

The rule *no longer* requires an issuer to disclose whether or not an audit committee *financial expert* is serving on its audit committee. Instead, issuers are required to describe, for each member of the audit committee, that member's education and experience that relate to his or her responsibilities as an audit committee member.

The *audit committee's responsibilities* must explicitly relate to the appointment, compensation, retention, and oversight of the external auditor, as well as to the pre-approval of all non-audit services to be provided by the external auditor. Audit committees must also have a written *charter*, and establish procedures to deal with *complaints* regarding accounting, internal accounting controls, or auditing matters and to deal with the *confidential*, anonymous *submission* by employees of *concerns* regarding questionable accounting or auditing matters.

Support of The Canadian Public Accountability Board: National Instrument 52–108

Financial statements of public companies will have to be audited only by a public accounting firm that is a participating audit firm with the Canadian Public Accountability Board (CPAB) and which is in compliance with any restrictions or sanctions imposed by the CPAB as of the date of the auditors' report.

The rule will also apply to foreign companies which are reporting issuers in Canada, requiring foreign audit firms to register with the CPAB (the deadline for foreign firms to register is July 19, 2004).

Best Practices for Effective Corporate Governance: Multilateral Policy 58–201

The proposed *recommended best practices* for all reporting issuers (corporate and non-corporate), which are *not* intended to be *prescriptive* and which have been mainly derived from the Toronto Stock Exchange corporate governance guidelines and the recently adopted listing standards of the NYSE, include:

◆ maintaining a *majority of independent directors* on the board of directors
  (a) *independent* will be defined to mean that a director has no direct or indirect *material relationship* with the issuer
  (b) *material relationship* will be defined to mean a relationship which could, in the view of the issuer's board, reasonably interfere with the exercise of a director's independent judgement, with certain individuals being deemed to have a material relationship with the issuer, and
  (c) in the case of *income trusts*, independence should occur at the trustee level, and, in the case of a *limited partnership*, independence should occur at the level of the board of directors of the general partner

◆ holding *separate*, regularly scheduled *meetings* of the *independent directors*

◆ appointing a *chair* of the board who is an *independent* director, or, if not appropriate, *a lead director who is* an *independent* director

◆ adopting a *written board mandate*, which should address matters such as integrity, strategic planning, managing risk, succession planning, corporate communications, required board approvals, internal controls, management information systems, and investor feedback

◆ developing *position* descriptions for *directors* (including for the chair of the board and of each board committee) and the *CEO*, including developing corporate goals and objectives that the CEO has to meet

◆ providing each new director with a comprehensive *orientation*, as well as providing all directors with *continuing education* opportunities

◆ adopting a written *code of business conduct and ethics*, applicable to directors, officers, and employees of the issuer, and monitored by the board (and which only the board may waive), reasonably designed *to deter wrongdoing* and which should address issues such as conflicts of interest, reporting illegal or unethical behaviour, and *fair dealing* with investors, customers, suppliers, competitors, and employees. Codes and waivers would be required to be disclosed

◆ appointing a *nominating committee* for directors composed *entirely* of *independent* directors, which should have a written *charter*

◆ considering the *appropriate size* of the board

◆ adopting a *process* for determining what *competencies and skills the board* as a whole should have, and those possessed by individual directors, and applying this result to the recruiting process of new directors

◆ appointing a *compensation committee* composed entirely of independent directors, with a written *charter*

◆ conducting *regular assessments* of *board effectiveness*, as well as the effectiveness and contribution of each board *committee* and each *individual director*.

Disclosure of Corporate Governance Practices: Multilateral Instrument 58–101

The proposed rule would establish both a disclosure requirement regarding corporate governance practices that the issuer has adopted, and a requirement to publicly file with the regulators any written code of business conduct and ethics (and any amendments) that the issuer may have adopted. Waivers (whether explicit or implicit) granted by the board from this code in favour of directors or officers would also have to be immediately disclosed via a press release.

The proposed rule applies to all reporting issuers, other than investment funds, issuers of asset-backed securities, designated foreign issuers, SEC foreign issuers, certain exchangeable security issuers, and certain credit support issuers.

Every issuer to whom the proposed rule applies, other than a venture issuer, must include in its AIF specific disclosure regarding: the composition of the board; the mandate of the board; the position descriptions for the chair, the chair of each committee and directors; measures adopted respecting the orientation and continuing education of directors; the adoption of a code of business conduct and ethics; the composition of the nomination committee and its mandate or other nomination process; the composition of the compensation committee and its mandate or other compensation process; and the assessment process for the performance of the board, of each committee of the board and of each board member.

As part of the disclosure, if the issuer does not meet the recommended best practices with respect to each disclosure item, the issuer would be required to explain why the board considers its practice appropriate.

Appendix D—Report and Certification Templates

The following pages provide templates for the required reports and certifications required by the Act.

These templates are intended as guides only, and they must be checked and revised before submission by the Audit Committee and/or the CFO to ensure compliance with the requirements of the particular document.

The main reason for this check and revise procedure is to ensure that recent and current changes or amendments to the Act have been incorporated.

A selection of templates referring to various Sections of the Act is also included. These templates are intended as a guide only, and each company should modify them to suit its own requirements.

The final Template offered is a Summary of SOX as it affects a company's suppliers, clients and others that the company does business with. These entities are affected to varying degrees by the company's efforts towards compliance with SOX requirements, and may feel resentment or frustration that their traditional methods of doing business with the company are being changed or made more complicated. Typically, the accounting aspects of the company/client/supplier relationship come under scrutiny and must be documented on an ongoing and accurate basis. This often means re-visiting such elements as Credit Applications, Payment Histories, or Deliveries and Returns Records. These elements are all important to a company since they directly affect the Risk Assessments throughout the company's internal control system. This template provides a simple summary that explains why a company's client/supplier is being asked to perform some task or change its way of doing business with the company.

Disclosure Certification

I,

certify that:

I have reviewed this   of   ;

Based on my knowledge, this report does not contain any untrue statement of a material fact or omit to state a material fact necessary to make the statements made, in light of the circumstances under which such statements were made, nor misleading with respect to the period covered by this report;

Based on my knowledge, the financial statements, and other financial information included in this report, fairly present in all material respects the financial condition, results of operations, and cash flows of the small business issuer as of, and for, the periods presented in this report;

The small business issuer's other certifying officer(s) and I are responsible for establishing and maintaining disclosure controls and procedures (as defined in Exchange Act Rules 13a-15(e) and 15d-15(e)) and internal control over financial reporting (as defined in Exchange Act Rules 13a-15(f) and 15d-15(f)) for the small business issuer and have:

(a) Designed such disclosure controls and procedures, or caused such disclosure controls and procedures to be designed under our supervision, to ensure that material information relating to the small business issuer, including its consolidated subsidiaries, is made known to us by others within those entities, particularly during the period in which this report is being prepared;

(b) Designed such internal control over financial reporting, or caused such internal control over financial reporting to be designed under our supervision, to provide reasonable assurance regarding the reliability of financial reporting and the preparation of financial statements for external purposes in accordance with generally accepted accounting principles;

(c) Evaluated the effectiveness of the small business issuer's disclosure controls and procedures and presented in this report our conclusions about the effectiveness of the disclosure controls and procedures, as of the end of the period covered by this report based on such evaluation; and

(d) Disclosed in this report any change in the small business issuer's internal control over financial reporting that occurred during the small business issuer's most recent fiscal quarter (the small business issuer's fourth fiscal quarter in the case of an annual report) that has materially affected, or is reasonably likely to materially affect, the small business issuer's internal control over financial reporting; and

The small business issuer's other certifying officer(s) and I have disclosed, based on our most recent evaluation of internal control over financial reporting, to the small business issuer's auditors and the audit committee of the small business issuer's board of directors (or persons performing the equivalent functions):

(a) All significant deficiencies and material weaknesses in the design or operation of internal control over financial reporting which are reasonably likely to adversely affect the small business issuer's ability to record, process, summarize, and report financial information; and

(b) Any fraud, whether or not material, that involves management or other employees who have a significant role in the small business issuer's internal control over financial reporting.

Date:

(Signature)

_____

　　　(Title)

This template and the others shown in this book are presented for your unlimited use in the CDROM attached to this book. They are in Microsoft Word Format and can easily be downloaded to your computer.

Disclosure Internal Control Report

Contents

Code of Ethics

I;   (name)   (position) will:

Embody and enforce this Code of Ethics.

Ensure that this Code of Ethics is communicated at least annually throughout all financial departments.

Formally and promptly communicate any breach of this Code of Ethics to the Senior Vice President and General Counsel.

Act at all times with honesty, integrity and independence, avoiding actual or apparent conflicts of interest in personal and professional relationships.

Discuss with the appropriate Senior Management level, or, in the case of the Chief Executive Officer, with the Senior Vice President and General Counsel, in advance, any transaction that reasonably could be expected to give rise to a conflict of interest.

Provide full, fair, accurate, complete, objective, timely and understandable financial disclosures in internal reports as well as documents filed or submitted to the Securities and Exchange Commission, any other government agency or self-regulatory organization, or used in public communications.

Comply with all applicable rules and regulations of federal, state, provincial and local governments, the Securities and Exchange Commission, the New York Stock Exchange and other exchanges on which the Company's stock is listed, and other appropriate private and public regulatory agencies.

Comply with the Company's policies and procedures.

Act in good faith, responsibly, with due care, competence, diligence, and without knowingly misrepresenting material facts or allowing my better judgment to be subordinated.

Protect and respect the confidentiality of information acquired in the course of my work except when authorized or otherwise legally obligated to disclose.

Confidential information acquired in the course of my work will not be used for personal advantage.

Be recognized as a responsible partner among my peers.

Responsibly use and control assets and other resources employed or entrusted to my supervision.

Signature: —————————————————————————

Date:

Accounting Firm Registration Acknowledgement

I/we hereby certify that the accounting firm of:

is duly and currently registered with the Public Company Accounting Oversight Board.

Signed:_____

Position:

Date:

AUDITING, QUALITY CONTROL, AND ETHICS STANDARDS

I/we hereby certify that the accounting firm of:

comply with the quality control and ethics rules of the Public Company Accounting Oversight Board.

Signed:_____

Position:

Date:

FOREIGN PUBLIC ACCOUNTING FIRMS

I/we hereby certify that the accounting firm of:

when performing audits or other accounting and/or auditing functions for the Company, does and will conform to the requirements of the Sarbanes–Oxley Act, and does and will conform to the quality control and ethics rules of the Public Company Accounting Oversight Board.

Signed:_____

Position:

Date:

ACCOUNTING STANDARDS

I/we hereby certify that the accounting firm of:

during the course of its business, utilizes generally acceptable accounting system(s) according to the requirements of the Sarbanes–Oxley Act. The system currently in use by the firm is:

Signed:_____

Position:

Date:

SERVICES OUTSIDE THE SCOPE OF PRACTICE OF AUDITORS

I/we hereby certify that the following activities are performed by the company or companies as noted below:

External Audits

Internal Audits (outsourced)

Bookkeeping/Accounting

Financial Information Systems Design & Implementation

Appraisal or valuation services, fairness opinions, or contribution-in-kind reports

Actuarial Services

Management Functions or Human Resources

Broker or dealer, investment adviser, or investment banking services

Legal services and expert services unrelated to an audit

Any other activities prohibited by the Public Company Accounting Oversight Board (define)

Signed:_____

Position:

Date:

AUDIT PARTNER ROTATION

I/we hereby certify that the following list of audit partners and the dates they performed audit functions on behalf of the Company represent a true record.

Partner

Firm

Fiscal Year: Fiscal Year: Fiscal Year: Fiscal Year: Fiscal Year:

Partner

Firm

Fiscal Year: Fiscal Year: Fiscal Year: Fiscal Year: Fiscal Year:

Partner

Firm

Fiscal Year: Fiscal Year: Fiscal Year: Fiscal Year: Fiscal Year:

Partner

Firm

Fiscal Year: Fiscal Year: Fiscal Year: Fiscal Year: Fiscal Year:

Partner

Firm

Fiscal Year: Fiscal Year: Fiscal Year: Fiscal Year: Fiscal Year:

Signed:_____

Position:

Date:

AUDITOR REPORTS TO AUDIT COMMITTEES

This Binder contains copies of all pertinent documents involving
discussions and decisions made between

(The Auditing Firm)

And the Company

During the period from   to:

Binder Number   of

AUDIT COMMITTEE

On behalf of the Company, the following individuals are appointed to perform the duties of the Audit Committee as defined in the Sarbanes–Oxley Act, and are required to perform their duties in a manner consistent with the requirements of the Act as it pertains to Audit Committees. The members of the Committee will appoint the Chairman of the Committee at their first meeting.

Name:

Firm (if independent of the Company)

Address:

Telephone (bus)   Telephone (res)   Telephone (cel)

e-mail

Appointment start date: Termination Date:

Name:

Firm (if independent of the Company)

Address:

Telephone (bus)   Telephone (res)   Telephone (cel)

e-mail

Appointment start date: Termination Date:

Name:

Firm (if independent of the Company)

Address:

Telephone (bus)   Telephone (res)   Telephone (cel)

e-mail

Appointment start date: Termination Date:

Sarbanes Oxley Compliance – Template 2.4

Name:

Firm (if independent of the Company)

Address:

Telephone (bus)   Telephone (res)   Telephone (cel)

e-mail

Appointment start date: Termination Date:

Name:

Firm (if independent of the Company)

Address:

Telephone (bus)   Telephone (res)   Telephone (cel)

e-mail

Appointment start date: Termination Date:

Name:

Firm (if independent of the Company)

Address:

Telephone (bus)   Telephone (res)   Telephone (cel)

e-mail

Appointment start date: Termination Date:

Signed:_____

Position:

Date:

COMPLAINTS OR CONCERNS

This form is to be used by a person or persons who wish to inform the Audit Committee of the Company of an incident, practice, action, attitude or any other factor which may affect the financial well-being of the Company and in particular may affect the validity, accuracy, and truthfulness of its financial reports and statements.

The information contained in this report will, at the request of the person presenting the information, remain in confidence by the Audit Committee, and the person submitting the complaint or concern shall remain anonymous. In no case will the person be punished or suffer any negative retribution or penalty by any member of the Audit Committee, management and officers of the Company, or other employee as a result of submitting this concern or complaint.

Date of Submission:

General Subject

Details:

Is there any documented or other physical evidence to support your concerns?

Is it readily available, and if so, how?

How do you feel the situation could be remedied?

Are there any specific recommendations you could make that would improve the job or activity performance so that problems do not occur in the future?

Do you want this submission to be kept confidential by the Committee?

Would you be prepared to appear before the Committee to discuss your concerns?

OPTIONAL:

Name: Position:

Telephone (work)   Telephone (home)   Telephone (cel)

e-mail:

Template 3.2

Overview for Suppliers and Clients

The Sarbanes–Oxley Act of 2002 was created to ensure full disclosure of the financial aspects of public corporations to avoid as much as possible the kind of cheating and poor corporate governance that rocked the business community in the few years prior to 2002. The Act is applicable to ALL companies that are listed on any US Stock Exchange and compliance is mandatory, not optional. Large fines and/or prison sentences are threatened to CEOs, CFOs and other executives for non-compliance.

Other companies also come under the SEC interpretation of the Act and to whom it applies and may be enforced. Accordingly, we have undertaken to become Sarbanes–Oxley (SOX) compliant in our company, and are in the process of implementing the requirements throughout. This is a very time-consuming, complex, and expensive process.

The main thrust of SOX lies in detailed and on-going tracking and control of any aspect of the company's operations that in any way affects its financial well-being. Obviously, this means just about everything a company does. The Act is very clear in demanding that an Internal Control System be established in the company and that it be continuously and rigorously monitored and audited both internally and independently.

In order to accomplish the objectives of compliance, we find it necessary to re-visit our relationships with our suppliers, our clients and others with whom we do business. In particular, the financial relationships require clarification and sometimes updating. Out-of-date agreements, contracts and understandings may need to be rewritten and signed by current management.

We appreciate that this may cause some inconvenience and time-consuming effort on the part of our associates, but it is both necessary and desirable that our relationships are clarified and documented.

We thank you for your understanding and cooperation and hope that we can continue to do business in the same spirit and with the same, or better, efficiency that we have enjoyed in the past.

Best Regards

Appendix E—Overview of SOX
Commercial Software Solutions

There are many commercial solutions to the problems of SOX compliance. They range from the extremely expensive to affordable (for small- to medium-sized companies) and some go beyond compliance to provide a comprehensive and very useful business model. Listed below are a few of the available solutions with a brief description and a link to their websites. Following the list is an overview of a typical solution to show how it works. (Appendix F)

It is unlikely that any of the SOX Solutions will actually provide a complete solution, one that addresses all the complex processes necessary for compliance. Most of these solutions are extensions or enhancements of existing software applications that have been modified or dressed up to address the SOX requirements that apply to their particular area of specialization. Which ones to acquire, is a big question and one that requires a careful look at the applications already in place in a company, what gaps there are, and which solution will best integrate your existing systems with your total SOX compliance needs. This will constitute a significant and very important project involving the Finance and Accounting Department, the IT Department, and the Internal Auditor(s).

The chart at the end of Chapter 2 shows an overview of the Internal Controls System requirements, and that, combined with the elements described in the COSO Framework, should provide a basis from which to start.

Following are a few companies providing various software solutions for SOX compliance. The descriptions are taken directly from their websites.

ACL Continuous Controls Monitoring

ACL Continuous Controls Monitoring (CCM) solutions provide an independent mechanism to automatically monitor internal controls' effectiveness in support of compliance with Sarbanes–Oxley section 404.

Using marketing-leading ACL monitoring and analytic technology, organizations can reduce the cost of compliance and minimize the financial risks stemming from controls gaps and weaknesses. By automating sophisticated analytics and embedding audit "best practices" in organizations' business operations, management receives timely notification of anomalies and control breaches, mitigating risks of ineffective or missing controls within application systems. With enhanced insight gained by comparing and analyzing data from different systems across the enterprise, management and audit teams gain independent assurance of the integrity of transactions underlying financial reporting.

The benefits of ACL CCM solutions include:

(a) *Independent testing of controls* – through transaction analysis at the source level
(b) *Timely notification to management of controls breakdowns* – an "early warning system" of compliance risk, enabling control weaknesses to be fixed before they are reported externally
(c) *Fraud reduction and improved risk management* – through identification of control gaps and weaknesses that can lead to error, abuse, and fraud
(d) *Improvements to efficiency and effectiveness* – with potential to increase profitability by containing costs, minimizing losses, and improving revenue collection
(e) *Extensibility to multiple end-to-end business processes* – with independent assurance of controls effectiveness and transaction integrity across the enterprise.

ACL CCM solutions enable organizations to continually test and monitor the internal controls within critical business processes. They apply automated, pre-defined analytic tests to critical control points within specific business process areas, mapped to the Committee of Sponsoring Organizations (COSO) internal controls framework. CCM solutions become part of day-to-day operations, enabling efficient, independent testing of business transactions for errors, exceptions, and controls weaknesses.

Run automatically on a continuous basis, ACL CCM solutions check and validate transactional data from any ERP (including SAP, Oracle, and PeopleSoft), mainframe system, or custom application, against control parameters and business rules. ACL CCM analytics identify suspicious activity, errors, segregation of duties issues, and exceptions that may be hidden within high volumes of transactions. Through an easy-to-use browser-based interface, management receives timely notification of control breaches, can quickly review quantified exposure of business risk, and can drill down to specific exceptions and transactions to resolve potential problems before they escalate. As a result, organizations can better assure compliance, contain costs, and minimize losses.

The extensible ACL CCM framework allows organizations to focus on those business processes that represent the greatest potential risk, easily adding CCM application modules to gain an increasingly comprehensive overview of control exposures within the enterprise. ACL CCM solutions provide assurance for a wide range of key business and compliance processes, including the purchase-to-payment cycle, billing and receivables, payroll, inventory management, and general ledger reconciliation.

http://www.acl.com/solutions/sarbanes-oxley.aspx

IBM Workplace for Business Controls and Reporting

IBM Workplace for Business Controls and Reporting is a solution designed to help companies manage and assess their business controls. The offering provides corporations with the ability to document, monitor, and test internal controls that can help manage financial reporting processes in a cost-effective and sustainable manner. Specifically, the version V 2.5, announced in January 2005 and went GA in February; allows organizations to help drive down the cost of control with new features to help manage organizational change, simplify testing and auditing, and help improve performance through an update option that ensures different departments have the most current data at their fingertips.

IBM Workplace for Business Controls and Reporting provides a platform to allow companies to move from compliance to control management and then to enterprise risk management. Through shifting from Compliance and Control Management to Enterprise Risk Management companies will be able to systematically introduce risk analysis to their decision-making processes to drive greater business value.

Benefits

Role-based solution provides a platform and a consistent, organized approach helping to gain visibility into internal controls to quickly identify issues and help mitigate risks.

Help address challenges in meeting new compliance requirements in the areas of financial controls and reporting such as Sarbanes–Oxley and other global regulations.

IBM's software experience and KPMG's advice and knowledge of internal controls creates a comprehensive offering.

Can help make it easier for people to communicate and collaborate with presence awareness, instant messaging, and Team Places for document version control.

Audit trails and archiving help to ensure process and document integrity.

Can take advantage of industry insights and knowledge of internal control processes and practices via leading third party Control Catalogs.

Solution from a single vendor that can be extended with other products from the IBM software portfolio such as: DB2 Records Manager, DB2 Document Manager, Websphere Portal and Lotus Workplace Collaborative Learning.

Business consulting and software services help you started quickly.

Extensive worldwide network of business partners to accommodate installations, data migration, customization for other regulatory requirements, process improvement consulting, training and ad hoc analytics/reporting.

http://www.lotus.com/products/product5.nsf/wdocs/bcghomepage

OpenPages SOX Express

OpenPages Sarbanes–Oxley Express (SOX Express) is an enterprise compliance management solution that reduces the time and resource costs associated with ongoing compliance for sections 302 and 404 of the Sarbanes–Oxley Act.

Sarbanes–Oxley Express combines powerful document and process management with flexible reporting capabilities in an extremely easy-to-use environment that enables CEOs, CFOs, and financial management officers to enforce internal controls.

For Sarbanes–Oxley section 404, SOX Express automates the design, documentation, review, approval, and testing of a company's internal controls framework. SOX Express provides a COSO-based risk management framework to shorten time-to-compliance and to expedite compliance audits.

For Sarbanes–Oxley section 302, SOX Express automates the survey process for financial disclosure certification in which individual process owners first provide sub-certification for their functional areas. Sub-certifications are then "rolled-up" throughout the organization and approved by managers at each business level. SOX Express then presents management with a final certification report for attestation from corporate officers.

With a browser-based interface and a standards-based architecture, SOX Express is rapidly installed and easily integrated into existing IT environments. Built on a Java-based web-services architecture, IT organizations will appreciate SOX Express' minimal impact on existing infrastructure and resources. Additionally, SOX Express can be configured by business users, helping to keep total cost of ownership low by eliminating the need for IT administration.

Because of its intuitive interface, consistent navigation, and format, SOX Express is extremely easy to use. Personalized, user-specific home pages make the user experience extremely efficient and ensures end-user adoption and productivity.

http://www.openpages.com/solutions/sarbanes-oxley/ sarbanes-oxley- express.asp

S–O Comply® Sarbanes–Oxley Compliance Application Software

onProject, Inc. has leveraged years of project management experience with 40,000 + companies as well as extensive audit methodology and risk assessment automation experience working with "Big Four" accounting firms to develop next generation audit tools for both internal use and in collaboration with their clients to offer S–O Comply, the multi-user resource software that enables companies to easily and affordably implement and monitor control activity.

S–O Comply will meet the needs of reporting companies that must enact "disclosure controls and procedures" in a collaborative, secure environment.

S–O Comply is flexible enough to meet the needs of the smallest or largest public companies. Since the product's introduction in April of 2003 **onProject** has secured thousands of users within these corporations. This continued success positions us as one of the leading software solutions for Sarbanes–Oxley compliance available today.

onProject has been recognized as a known or preferred SOX software vendor by the Big Four accounting firms, CFO Magazine®, AICPA and Gartner, Inc.

S–O Comply is available in two versions:

Enterprise—A Client-Server/Web model providing a rich graphical interface and tools for performing complex, cross-organizational operations.

Small Group—For those companies where few users are required and few organization structures exist. The same features and functionality of the enterprise but for the desktop.

http://www.onproject.com/soa/

REPORT2WEB   Redwood's Sarbanes–Oxley Software Solutions

The Sarbanes–Oxley Act of 2002 has heightened the standards for financial reporting dramatically. Redwood's Sarbanes–Oxley compliance solutions help companies to manage risk by providing tools for internal controls, general IT controls, information and communications, and monitoring. Redwood's Sarbanes–Oxley solutions not only help companies build a sustainable compliance solution, but also provide business value by streamlining operations and automating manual processes.

Current compliance projects are assisted by Redwood document management tools which assist during the documentation, remediation and testing phases, including management of Microsoft Word, Excel, and Visio documents.

By providing a secure repository of documents produced by any application or platform, Redwood Solutions enable business managers and auditors to pinpoint the information they need regardless of source.

Redwood Sarbanes–Oxley solutions provide automation of general IT controls for job scheduling and business process control and monitoring across. These general IT control solutions are tightly integrated with ERP systems such as SAP, and can handle the most complex multi-application and multi-platform computing environments.

Internal controls for information capture and access, segmentation of duties, document alteration protection and document retention are provided by Redwood Sarbanes–Oxley solutions. Internal controls for period-end close are essential to accurate, reliable financial reporting. Redwood's event-driven job scheduling and information distribution products enable tight monitoring and control over period-end close processes, and alerts and notifications of irregularities in either the business processes or the documentation produced during the close.

Report2Web is a Web-based document management solution that enables organizations to securely publish, store, and deliver documents online. Hundreds of organizations depend on Report2Web each day to improve the efficiency and reduce the latency of communications, internally and to external business partners and customers. With no need to modify existing applications, Report2Web captures, organizes, and stores documents in a centralized repository, extracts meaningful information, and automates the delivery of personalized content to individuals.

http://www.redwood.com/information/sarbanes_oxley_software.htm.

Movaris® Certainty™ SOX Software for Financial Control Management

Movaris Certainty is easy-to-use, web-based, enterprise-class Sarbanes–Oxley software that addresses the key challenges of ongoing compliance, beyond the initial documentation effort. However, Certainty is more than just Sarbanes–Oxley software. While managing all phases of compliance, Certainty also creates a foundation for strong financial control to manage compliance day-to-day.

In addition, Certainty provides a solid financial control management environment for any company, including public and private companies, and not-for-profit organizations.

Certainty **documents** financial controls, provides a comprehensive **testing and review** environment, initiates pre-built action plans designed to **improve** the control environment, and produces necessary compliance **reports** for Sarbanes–Oxley Section 404 and Section 302 on demand. Combined, these four phases create an environment that enforces accountability across the entire enterprise, and reduces the time and costs of ongoing compliance, year after year.

Designed specifically to address enterprise-wide Sarbanes–Oxley compliance and financial control management, Movaris Certainty Sarbanes–Oxley software:

Reduces and continuously contains out-of-pocket costs.

Reduces time-to-compliance with quick implementation and minimal training requirements.

Activates financial controls to strengthen the effectiveness of financial operations.

Expands and scales as business conditions change and the financial control environment broadens and matures.

Incorporates changes in the regulatory environment, new PCAOB interpretations, and pronouncements.

Overcomes organizational and geographical barriers to enforce compliance policies.

Creates a complete body of evidence for all phases of documentation, review, improvement, and attestation with:

context searches
pre-built reports
ad hoc analyses
audit walk-through paths

Capabilities of Certainty Sarbanes–Oxley Software

Internal Control Documentation
Review of Internal Controls and Internal Control Testing
Financial Risk Assessment and Control Environment Improvements
Asserting and Reporting

http://www.movaris.com/product/index.html.

Certus Governance Suite

The Certus Governance Suite consists of three tightly integrated software modules which operate on a powerful compliance platform.

Our flagship product modules, Certus 404 and Certus 302, provide a robust, comprehensive solution to help companies meet their most pressing Sarbanes–Oxley compliance requirements quickly and easily. The Certus Governance Suite is also accompanied by implementation services dedicated to the rapid deployment and cost-effective maintenance of the software, and ultimately to the success of your project.

Comprehensive Software for Sustainable Compliance

The Certus Governance Suite addresses all aspects of your Sarbanes–Oxley compliance efforts, including content, process and project workflow, communication management and documentation. Through a single, integrated platform, the Certus suite ensures scalability and consistency to minimize deployment costs and enable companies to build a sustainable practice that is easy to maintain.

With the Certus Governance Suite, you can:

design internal controls
evaluate operational effectiveness
monitor the progress of your compliance project
report on governance status and trends

As a result, the software provides management with greater visibility into control status and risks—giving your company a single source of truth. The software also offers users the option to manage audit plans and walkthroughs, thereby helping you minimize total compliance costs.

The Certus Governance Suite is also designed to help you leverage your compliance software environment to support other governance initiatives. For Sarbanes–Oxley compliance, the Certus suite provides best practice toolkits including control frameworks such as COSO, COBIT, and SOX templates from the "Big 4" accounting and auditing firms. The software can also be used to track compliance beyond Sarbanes–Oxley, with other regulatory efforts such as country-specific financial control regulations.

http://www.certus.com/products/governance_suite.html.

CARDMap SOX/Operational Risk and Enterprise Risk Management

Overview

CARD®map software is designed to help organizations meet risk and control governance responsibilities including Sarbanes–Oxley and the emerging Basel II operational risk requirements.

It is an easy-to-learn, easy-to-use Web-enabled software program that charts and monitors any facet of an organization's operation. It is a systematic approach that allows users to create an accurate and up-to-date survey of objectives, risks, controls, and residual risk status. It identifies problems, monitors process performance, assigns responsibility, and prioritizes action items. Over time, an integrated database of loss history, risk exposures, controls, residual risk status, action plans, and quality assurance work for an entire organization is built.

Highlights include:

Reporter fields that alert and allow senior management to monitor significant control and risk issues and problems.

Robust assessment scheduling capabilities and reminder calendars—particularly important for SOX 302 and 404.

Ability to assign accountability for risk/control assessments, action plans, and quality assurance work for SOX 404 audits and regulatory reviews.

High impact, drill down graphs, and custom reports.

Ability to attach working papers and other documents directly or via URL links.

Control and risk model flexibility – COSO 1992, COSO ERM 2004, CoCo, customized versions.

Features

CARDmap is built on the central premise that everyone within an organization, including work units, senior management and the board of directors, as well as internal and external assurance specialists should work together to provide assurances to key stakeholders that the controls in place within the organization result in an acceptable level of residual risk related to the achievement of business objectives.

Full support for SOX section 302 and 404 and Basel II operational risk management requirements.

Summary screens and graphs that shows senior executives at a glance the location and specifics on all serious internal control problems, especially significant deficiencies and material weaknesses.

Easy-to-use input forms with pop-up explanations to encourage work units to actively participate in the risk and control assessment and design.

Features to allow internal assurance specialists including internal auditors, compliance groups, and risk and insurance personnel to integrate their verification and quality assurance work with assessment work done by work units.

A Loss Event database that provides support for the new event identification category in COSO ERM 2004.

Loss Event/Risk Scenario Modeling that allows for users to input plausible risk situations and identify where, if at all, the risk scenario has been addressed by the organization—an important requirement in the Basel operational risk area and useful in any organization.

Residual Risk Index Electronic Signature Verification provides an audit trail of management's responsibility for and confirmation of the residual risk status on all objectives.

The Control Trigger Question feature helps users identify all the controls in use/place to manage risk. This feature can be customized.

The Control Verification Electronic Signature places responsibility for reporting on control status with the business units. It indicates how many of the hundreds of controls are actually functioning as described.

http://www.paisleyconsulting.com/website/pcweb.nsf#comp

BMC Software "REMEDY" IT Control System

The Sarbanes–Oxley Act of 2002 will have a significant impact on IT organizations. In accordance with Sarbanes Oxley (Sarbox), executives must attest to the adequacy and effectiveness of their internal controls, including IT controls. Therefore, IT controls will be externally audited, and a statement of control verified by the audit must now appear in annual reports filed with the Securities and Exchange Commission (SEC).

Companies must identify their significant financial accounts, the business processes that support those financial accounts, and the applications and IT systems that support those business processes. Then they must document and test controls at the financial process level, the application level, and the IT infrastructure level.

Although Sarbox does not mandate automated systems-based controls, such controls may ease the compliance process. Auditors will be looking not only for process consistency, but also for the consistent use of controls over those processes. For this reason, auditors may be more critical of manual or paper-based processes in large or distributed organizations. In many cases, using software solutions, such as those from BMC Software, is the best way to implement consistent controls.

Specifically, Remedy IT Service Management Solutions for the Enterprise can help automate and control IT processes that auditors will review. Because, in general, auditors will not probe as hard when they see that applications are consistently being utilized; you can help to accelerate the audit process by automating your IT processes.

Mapping Remedy Solutions to IT Controls

As part of the preparation for a Sarbox IT audit, an IT control framework must be identified. COBIT, an IT control framework recognized by the audit community, provides a comprehensive set of control objectives that an auditor may follow point-by-point during an audit.

To support Sarbox, the IT Governance Institute has released an adaptation of COBIT that specifies different process areas that an IT auditor may assess in the context of a Sarbanes–Oxley IT audit.

To understand which of these must be demonstrated to pass the audit, consult with your company's auditor. In addition, as you prepare for your Sarbox audit, consider how software solutions can help to support the following COBIT control objectives:

Accelerated Sarbox Compliance

Using Remedy software solutions to manage audited operations helps accelerate Sarbanes–Oxley compliance. Companies already using Remedy IT Service Management for the Enterprise can use these solutions as the basis for process and control documentation to facilitate compliance with Sarbanes–Oxley. For companies seeking solutions to improve current processes to meet audit requirements, Remedy solutions can be implemented quickly to achieve stable and consistent processes before audit activities begin.

http://www.remedy.com/solutions/best_practices/sarbox/index.html.

Processes On Demand Sarbanes–Oxley IT Process

Processes On Demand is a Sarbanes–Oxley compliant IT Process that provides a complete intranet/LAN ready HTML based software solution that enables PMOs and virtual PMOs to rapidly set up, use, and continuously improve upon their core processes and best practices. Processes On Demand meets the project management process, classification, documentation, process integration, decision criteria, and risk management requirements for Sarbanes–Oxley section 302, 404, and 409 compliance.

Sarbanes–Oxley IT Process—Value Proposition

Processes On Demand provided us with SOX compliant project management processes for PMBOK®, SDLC, and Change Management that work with the IT infrastructure and project management products that we already have and know, and at a fraction of the time and cost of other vendor alternatives—VP of IT.

We have helped many customers with our project management process software. SOX compliant PMBOK®, SDLC, and Change Management processes were set up in 3 days and for 75% less than other vendor proposals—Bernie Keh, President, BOT International

What you Need and What you can Expect

Clearly documented processes that meet the **"Project Control and Reporting"** requirements of the Sarbanes–Oxley Act (US).

Verifiable, auditable, and usable process solution on your intranet/ LAN infrastructure that meets the **"Evidence"** requirements of your Sarbanes–Oxley audit.

Improved project performance, consistency, and repeatability across all projects.

Continuous improvement and organizational maturity.

Knowledge sharing and skills transfer among project participants.

Easy integration with existing IT infrastructure (intranet/LAN) and user applications, such as Microsoft® Office, Microsoft Project, etc.

Compliance Requirement	Support of Compliance
Process: Implement a standard project management process to establish control processes and activities associated with scope, cost, and schedule.	Processes On Demand comes with a ready-to-use, proven project management process aligned to de factor standard approaches such as PMBOK® and SDLC. Processes On Demand provides a Process Builder for tailoring of additional and organization unique processes and reporting requirements.
Classification: Establish a project category or classification scheme that includes all projects associated or impacted with Sarbanes–Oxley compliance.	Processes On Demand provides project classification schemes. Projects associated with or impacted by Sarbanes–Oxley can be tracked and managed.
Documentation: Thoroughly document any changes that are made to financial systems as a result of associated IT or financial based projects.	Processes On Demand provides templates and checklists for tracking and managing changes.
Process Integration: For projects affecting any financial related system, ensure that good product and project development processes are followed.	Processes On Demand provides project and product development processes. Project management processes are integrated with product development life cycles such as product Go-to-Market (GTM) and software development life cycle (SDLC) and incorporated into the Processes On Demand.
Decision Criteria: Establish a standard stage-gate approach for all projects.	Processes On Demand provides process gates and stages, as well as reporting requirements and presentation templates. In addition, project scorecard criteria and criteria for a "go/no go" decision on projects are provided.
Risk Management: Define a risk management process that can be used to identify risks early, and to plan mitigation strategies.	Processes On Demand provides risk management and quality management processes. Workflows, process descriptions, templates, forms, and checklists are provided to identify risks and plan mitigation strategies.

Though the majority of the Sarbanes–Oxley Act of 2002 is associated with public accounting, auditing, internal controls, and financial reporting, sections 302, 404, and 409 are written specifically to address project management and Information Technology related project and process activities. Processes On Demand helps your organization address the essential project management actions that need to be taken to ensure compliance down to the project level.

http://www.botinternational.com/sarbanes_oxley_it_process.htm

MetricStream Corporate Governance Software

The Sarbanes–Oxley Act puts the responsibility for financial reporting accuracy and compliance with all applicable laws squarely on the desks of the CEO, the CFO, and the board of directors. Careers, stock valuations, and net worth are at stake.

Section 404 of the Sarbanes–Oxley Act goes beyond financial statement certification, and for the first time mandates new governance and tighter operational controls. Corporations now face a daunting challenge in documenting all critical operational controls, assessing the effectiveness of these controls over financial reporting, and subjecting the assessment report to the scrutiny of independent auditors.

MetricStream enables companies to effectively comply with the Sarbanes–Oxley Act and manage financial reporting risks. It provides complete end-to-end functionality for initial and ongoing compliance with Section 404 of the Sarbanes–Oxley Act. Using MetricStream, companies can design, assess, improve, and monitor processes and internal controls over financial reporting. The solution proactively schedules, notifies, and tracks all activities for appropriate contributors within all business units. The solution provides greater control and visibility to management and improves internal business processes.

Key Capabilities of MetricStream Sarbanes–Oxley 404 suite include:

Design and Document Internal Controls: Using MetricStream, organizations can cost-effectively design and document key processes, objectives, risks, and internal controls. The documentation is performed in accordance with the COSO framework. The solution also enables organizations to setup their compliance environment. Significant processes, financial statement accounts, management assertions, and all reference documentation can be identified. Assessment plans to test the design effectiveness and the operational effectiveness of the control structure can be defined. MetricStream can also import documentation residing in other systems or what have already been completed using office automation tools.

Assess Effectiveness of Internal Controls: The assessment of internal controls is at the core of compliance. Using MetricStream, organizations can schedule and perform assessments of design effectiveness and operational effectiveness of the controls. Appropriate scores are assigned for the assessments and ongoing and quarterly results can be reported.

Remedy Issues: It is critical for organizations to remedy all issues identified during the assessments. MetricStream enables the organization to manage remediation processes and implement remediation action plans. All other exceptions, issues, deficiencies, and material weaknesses identified can also be tracked and appropriate disclosures for all stakeholders can be generated.

Provide Visibility: Visibility into the status of the compliance effort is critical to management, auditors, process owners, and other stakeholders. MetricStream offers packaged reports, charts, and dashboards that provide relevant and timely visibility into the entire Sarbanes–Oxley compliance effort for all stakeholders.

Information and Communication: MetricStream also offers additional document management, training management, and audit management features. These can be used to track and notify the appropriate users about updates to the organization's policies, procedures, and other compliance-related documentation. When necessary appropriate training programs can be developed and conducted for all the impacted users. Audit management can perform process-level self-assessments and provide support for internal and external auditors.

http://www.metricstream.com/products/sarboxly.htm?channel= metricstream%20website.

Microsoft Office System-based Sarbanes–Oxley Solutions

While Microsoft does not have a specific Sarbanes–Oxley solution, the Microsoft Office System is a rich platform that customers and partners can use as a foundation for building solutions that address Sarbanes–Oxley challenges.

It can help manage compliance initiatives related to sections 302 and 404 of the Sarbanes–Oxley Act more efficiently.

Sarbanes–Oxley solutions built on the Microsoft Office System give you more visibility into financial processes and controls to help you comply with government regulations and have better oversight of corporate activities.

Challenges

Business expectations have changed dramatically since the Sarbanes–Oxley Act of 2002 was passed in July 2002. Companies are held to a new level of accountability, and executives are challenged to:

- Meet requirements of Sarbanes–Oxley sections 302 and 404
- Demonstrate financial transparency and good corporate governance to investors
- Implement a system for managing compliance initiatives
- Maintain focus on core organizational missions.

The Sarbanes–Oxley Act is not just a one-time compliance exercise. It is a new way of doing business that will force executives to anticipate risk and manage it carefully.

Sarbanes–Oxley solutions built on the Microsoft Office System can help your company efficiently manage the extensive work required to comply with sections 302 and 404 of the Sarbanes–Oxley Act. Building solutions on familiar Microsoft technologies makes them intuitive for users across an organization.

With Sarbanes–Oxley solutions built on the Microsoft Office System, you can:

- Provide real-time visibility into processes, risks, and controls from a single point of access
- Manage and use information to effectively make decisions—not just collect data

- Reduce costs by facilitating and accelerating the compliance process
- Establish a flexible foundation for longer-term compliance initiatives.

Core Capabilities

The Microsoft Office System offers the following functionality on which to build your solution:

- Document and information management. Provide intelligent information storage, categorization, and search with Extensible Markup Language (XML) data structuring and a familiar user interface.
- Process automation and workflow. Give employees the appropriate alerts, materials, and routing information needed to initiate and complete tasks.
- Communication and collaboration. Enable timely information sharing between employees, task assignments, and document versioning to make it easier to collaborate on projects.
- Monitoring and reporting. Provide dashboards and reports to monitor project status and enable access to critical data for real-time decision-making.
- System documentation and administration tools. Migrate data from existing Sarbanes–Oxley tools, review system architecture documentation, and use tools to effectively maintain and operate your solution.

http://www.microsoft.com/office/showcase/default.mspx

HandySoft SOXA Accelerator—Sarbanes–Oxley Compliance and Enterprise Risk Management

SOXA Accelerator, built-in partnership with Plumtree Software, provides the capabilities public companies need to establish the rigorous internal controls and reporting procedures that the Sarbanes–Oxley Act of 2002 demands. The unique combination of BizFlow's capabilities for process design, automation, reporting, and monitoring, along with Plumtree's collaboration, content management, search and personalization, make this the ideal solution for complying with stringent regulations.

Project & Task Management – Define Significant Accounts/
Functions, Processes, Risks, and Internal Controls that conform
to standards such as the COSO framework

Personalized Views – Give each member of the extended accounting
and compliance team a personalized view of the compliance
process and assigned tasks

Dashboard Views – Provide pre-built, third-party dashboard views
for graphical, color-coded drill-down reporting

302 & 404 Rollup and Certification – Streamline and automate 302
and 404 rollup and certification for monitoring, approval, and
certification of the state of internal controls

Centralized Documentation – Automate the gathering of documentation and evidence needed for compliance

Secure Collaboration – Internal finance groups and external
accounting agencies collaborate on documentation and processes

Automated Workflows – Automate issue management and document sign-off

Issue Management – Identify issues and improvement opportunities
in your assessment, monitoring, and internal control processes

Data Integrity – Ensure protection of data and documentation with
audit trails, document management, version control, and security
measures

Real-time Reporting – Deliver insights into the status and performance of controls

http://www.handysoft.com/solutions/sarbanes-oxley/

Amadeus Corporate Governance Management Solutions

Manage effectively your management systems and remain compliant

Triggered by the important volatility of world markets, and fuelled
by the increasing number of world-class businesses declaring
bankruptcy, public and private corporations compliant with gov-
ernmental regulations such as Sarbanes–Oxley Act (SOX) in the
USA or Bill C-198 in Canada, are being pressured to come under
government regulations to substantiate and disclose their accounting practices. These regulations require that high-ranking corporate
officials, including the CFO and CEO, be held accountable for the
accuracy of their company's financial information.

The Amadeus Corporate Governance Management Software Solutions help your business meet the important challenges imposed by positioning efficient Corporate Governance, giving you full control of your compliance management infrastructure.

In order to assist you in achieving your goals, Amadeus Solutions incorporate the following powerful features: knowledge management, change management, auditing and evaluation of financial practices and processes management, training management, non-conformance management, corrective and preventive action management, consultant evaluations, objectives and criteria management and generate management reports. These advanced functionalities, combined with the Business Intelligence portal, insure that you efficiently operate your business, while benefiting from lower direct and indirect Corporate Governance compliance costs.

The value of Amadeus Solutions ultimately lies in their ability to help businesses achieve a high level of compliance.

Benefits of using Amadeus Corporate Governance Management Software Solutions:

◆ Insurance that all submissions have been reviewed and approved by all high-ranking levels before signing-off on consolidated results.
◆ Automation of the collection and the centralization of necessary documents and evidence needed to prove compliance.
◆ Insurance of record integrity with audit trails, document management, version control, and security measures ensuring data and document protection functionalities.
◆ Authentication, permission setting and complete support for managing digital signatures.
◆ Detection of potential problems and improvement opportunities for auditing and internal control processes.
◆ Secure collaboration between internal finance groups and external accounting agencies.
◆ Real-time monitoring and reporting allowing efficient monitoring of status and performance compliance.

http://www.amadeussolutions.com/english/solutions/corporate_governance.htm#.

CONCUR—Maximizing Control And Compliance

The cost of doing business just went up. The effects of the Sarbanes–Oxley Act continue to ripple throughout corporate America. Section 404 of the Act mandates that adequate "internal controls" exist to ensure compliance. CEOs must certify their financial results. Shareholders are demanding accountability. And the SEC now has the tools and resources at their disposal to police compliance issues.

And of course, it is not just public companies that are affected by the need for internal controls. Consider these statistics from The Association of Certified Fraud Examiners:

Fact 1: 45% of all companies experience fraud;

Fact 2: 22.1% of all fraud schemes are related to expense reimbursement;

Fact 3: The median cost of each fraud incidence is $60,000 (up from $20,000 in 1996);

Supporting Sarbanes–Oxley Compliance Through Concur Expense Service

Concur Expense Service makes it easy to identify and prevent fraud within the expense reporting process. By delivering the control, visibility and fraud intelligence every organization needs, Concur enables companies to rapidly comply with Sarbanes–Oxley section 404. The following chart illustrates the specific areas where Concur Expense Service features provide customers with the support they need for compliance.

Concur Expense Service Product Function/Feature	Supports these Areas		
	Control	Visibility	Fraud Intelligence
Best Practices Policy	X		
Work Flow	X	X	
Audit Rules	X		
Multiple Policy Administration	X		
Business Intelligence			
- Internal Control Reports	X	X	
- T&E Spend Management	X	X	X
Hosted Services	X		
Professional Services			
- Deployment	X		
- Documentation	X	X	
- Post Deployment Checkup	X	X	X
- Fraud Detection, Prevention Analysis			
Concur Imaging Service	X	X	
Archiving Reporting Data Mart	X	X	
Fraud Finder Tools			X

Compliance is just one reason to automate your expense reporting system. If you value streamlined operations, unprecedented visibility into your company's spending patterns, and rapid, maximized ROI, then Corporate Expense Management should be high on your agenda.

http://www.concur.com/solutions/value/compliance/default.asp.

CARTESIS—Sarbanes–Oxley Compliance

Overview

Sarbanes–Oxley has not made life any easier for finance executives. The list of requirements is staggering, and failure to integrate ongoing compliance into BPM processes and systems can be risky. Sarbanes–Oxley compliance is not a one-time hurdle to overcome— it is an ongoing process that must be constantly monitored, managed, and improved. CFOs need a BPM solution that promotes the consistency of financial data for all stakeholder groups, ensures the completeness and accuracy of that data as well as continually monitors the effectiveness of internal controls relating to SOX compliance.

Key Questions

◆ Can compliance metrics and a "compliance snapshot" be obtained in the current reporting environment?

◆ Are manual and low value-added processes automated, enabling more stringent reporting deadlines to be met?

◆ Are validation routines and controls embedded throughout BPM systems to ensure consistency, accuracy and, ultimately, data integrity?

◆ Can financial, non-financial, and compliance metrics be tracked from source to disclosure with total visibility, traceability, and auditability?

◆ Does all financial stakeholder information come from a single application?

Can compliance metrics and a "compliance snapshot" be obtained in the current reporting environment?

Compliance requires extensive, ongoing documentation of controls. The **Cartesis Suite** can incorporate a custom or COSO-based framework into internal controls reporting to capture compliance data throughout the global enterprise. Finance staff can then view a "compliance snapshot" at any time to identify weak spots in the organization down to the process level within a specific entity. Cartesis empowers CFOs to have confidence in the effectiveness of their control systems when filing all-important attestation reports to external auditors using the same system that manages their financial data.

Are manual and low value-added processes automated, enabling more stringent reporting deadlines to be met?

The key to disclosure speed is to automate manual activities in all BPM processes, such as inter-company transaction matching, recurring journals and report generation, as well as integrating data links to source systems. The Cartesis Suite provides workflow features that give finance managers visibility into bottlenecks and slow points during budgeting, closing, forecasting, or compliance reporting—all within a single and secure BPM system.

Are validation routines and controls embedded throughout BPM systems to ensure consistency, accuracy and, ultimately, data integrity?

The headaches involved with managing off-line spreadsheets and disparate systems are a thing of the past, as Cartesis automates data collection from disparate source systems and general ledgers. Finance managers are able to monitor all BPM processes and data generated by those processes with absolute visibility and confidence, enabling speed with unprecedented control. With processing checks and controls embedded throughout the solution, compliance is woven into every financial management process.

Can financial, non-financial, and compliance metrics be tracked from source to disclosure with total visibility, traceability, and auditability?

Certifying the completeness, accuracy, and integrity of reporting data as mandated in SOX section 302 is one of the biggest challenges of ongoing compliance. Since CFOs must now personally sign-off on financial reports, putting their professional reputations at risk, absolute confidence in the numbers is critical. The Cartesis Suite provides unmatched audit features like comprehensive trace and audit reports to give management visibility into how, when, by whom, and how much data has been changed. A multilevel security system allows multiple user groups, including external auditors, to gain "tailored" access to any area or data set while not compromising system security.

Does all financial stakeholder information come from a single application?

The Cartesis Suite satisfies all stakeholder needs in a single BPM solution, making "one version of the truth" a reality. With a single integrated data model, the Cartesis Suite provides the organization with room to grow as additional requirements emerge without the need for additional investment. Multiple categories of data—budget, actual, forecast, SEC, GAAP, IAS—can be pulled from a single data store, reducing the need for vast reconciliations prior to disclosure and greatly reducing the risk of restatements, omissions, or errors.

http://global.cartesis.com/index.php/products/5

VERITAS Software

VERITAS Software, one of the ten largest software companies in the world, is a leading provider of software and services to enable utility computing. In a utility computing model, IT resources are aligned with business needs and business applications are delivered with optimal performance and availability on top of a shared computing infrastructure, minimizing hardware and labor costs. With 2004 revenue of $2.04 billion, VERITAS delivers products and services for data protection, storage and server management, high availability and application performance management that are used by 99 percent of the Fortune 500.

Regulatory Readiness: Gain a Competitive Compliance Advantage with VERITAS

Every business wants a competitive advantage, especially facing the current and particularly challenging global economic climate. In light of the Enron and WorldCom collapse, and the subsequent introduction of new corporate compliance regulations including Sarbanes–Oxley, corporations are forced to recognize the reality of new regulatory constraints imposed on all facets of a business. It is no longer enough to find a competitive advantage. Now you must prove and document that your business practices, accounting methods, and competitive practices are in compliance with a host of complex, evolving regulations.

For the IT professional, the impact of regulatory compliance cannot be ignored and should not be minimized. Every audit request and every compliance requirement can potentially demand the attention and resources of IT and can seriously impact your ability to maintain enterprise-wide performance, availability, and reliability.

With thousands of different foreign and national regulatory regulations in force, IT administrators must take the initiative and establish strategies to ensure against inefficiencies and downtime brought on by regulatory audits and compliance requirements. The resourceful IT professional will work with corporate compliance officers to understand regulatory requirements and successfully establish compliance initiatives as insurance in case of audits. Because the IT component of compliance centers on the tracking, management, and retrieval of content, it is most logically and effectively implemented by IT administrators as an extension of data protection policies and plans. As the leader in data protection and management, VERITAS can be a key asset in your efforts to strengthen and streamline your compliance initiatives.

Formula for Regulatory Success: For the vast majority of businesses, compliance officers do not understand the IT domain and associated issues. Therefore, as an IT professional, you must find the IT compliance insurance policy that meets IT's criteria for your corporation. Any meaningful compliance solution must offer the following:

– It must recognize and address all relevant provisions of a regulatory code
– It must accommodate multiple regulatory protocols
– It must recognize, differentiate, and accommodate national and foreign regulatory codes
– It must accommodate revisions and additions to the relevant regulatory codes
– It must be data-type independent (compliance and audit requirements address more then just e-mail)
– It must allow for transparent marking and tracking of all content types
– It must store and relocate data in a manner consistent with IT storage, backup, and retrieval specifications
– It must be automated
– It must enable fast and efficient data retrieval

In addition, the most effective compliance solution should be two-tiered so that both compliance professionals and IT administrators can independently configure their respective components. Each tier should include a separate interface so both a compliance officer and an IT administrator have 24 × 7 × 365 access without requiring the other's participation or assistance. In this way, the corporate compliance officer can update and revise corporate regulatory policies without engaging the IT department, and you can satisfy IT's regulatory requirements — running audits, for example — without concern for regulatory policy configuration.

Regardless of how robust, configurable, and flexible your regulatory solution may be for your corporate compliance officer, it must be automated, fast, and unobtrusive to work for IT administrators. If the solution is manual and cumbersome, IT resources will be unnecessarily diverted from other enterprise priorities, leaving you and your enterprise exposed to performance degradation and reduced availability. The company that recognizes this and identifies the best automated solution clearly has a competitive edge.

To guarantee this efficiency, the astute IT professional will adopt a compliance solution that acts as an extension of the existing storage, backup, and data protection architecture. Using the features inherent in this particular suite of tools, an integrated compliance solution will exploit the archival, retrieval, and management functionality of that suite. As the industry leader in storage and data protection tools, VERITAS understands the complementary nature of compliance and data protection tools. For example, with VERITAS NetBackup, IT administrators can identify document characteristics across a heterogeneous enterprise, relocate or real-locate more suitable and economical storage resources for those particular documents, and move the documents accordingly. This process is fully automated, transparent to users, and reflects the core functionality of a compliance solution.

Finally, the ideal compliance solution must be data-type independent. While recent widely publicized corporate audits appear to have focused on e-mail, a compliance solution focusing exclusively or primarily on e-mail tracking, marking, and retrieval will prove to be woefully inadequate. The level of sophistication and breadth of today's audits continues to expand. Regulators want to have access to all relevant documents and files — regardless of format or data type — demanding a compliance initiative that recognizes and takes all content and file types into account.

Compliance as Competitive Advantage

As time goes by, the number of regulatory agencies and their associated regulations will continue to expand. Therefore, corporations must be prepared for and respond to increasingly complex regulatory audits. To do so effectively — without diverting precious IT resources — you will need a compliance solution that is fast, flexible, fully automated, and integrated with your storage and data protection architecture.

Such integration with VERITAS storage and data protection tools is ideal. At the forefront of the storage and data protection marketplace, VERITAS software tools offer the leverage you need to implement an exceptional compliance and regulatory solution. Although compliance and regulatory audits are not typically associated with a competitive advantage, implementing a VERITAS-based compliance solution affords you just such an advantage. With full automation, exceptional audit turnaround times, and well-established storage and data protection tools from VERITAS, you can be responsible for a regulatory and compliance initiative that delivers a competitive advantage, and ensures peace of mind in the event of a compliance audit.

www.veritas.com. "When you get to this site, type in Sarbanes Oxley in the advanced search field and click 'search'".

Appendix F—Overview of the
BOT International "Processes on
Demand" Software Solution

There are great differences between companies, not just in size, or complexity, but in the systems that they already use to provide a measure of control of their operations. It is easy to see, then, that to find a single, all-embracing solution for SOX compliance is difficult, if not impossible. In this book, we have seen that the actual require- ment as stated in sections 302, 404, and 409 are quite general in nature and so leave it up to the company to decide what is neces- sary to satisfy the enforcement of the Act.

The COSO Framework as described has been widely accepted as the basis for setting up Internal Control Systems, and its metho- dology closely resembles Project Management scenarios. The basic methods applied to project management should work for SOX compliance – in most cases.

That is why I have chosen to profile the "Processes-On-Demand" software as an example of compliance software available commer- cially. It is by no means the only applicable system available, and the people who have the job of deciding which system to use must do their own due diligence before embarking on the time- consuming and expensive process of becoming SOX compliant.

BOT International

> Processes On Demand is a Sarbanes–Oxley compliant IT Process that provides a complete intranet/LAN ready HTML based software solution that enables PMOs (Project Management Offices) and vir- tual PMOs to rapidly set up, use, and continuously improve upon their core processes and best practices. Processes On Demand meets the project management process, classification, documentation, process integration, decision criteria, and risk management require- ments for Sarbanes–Oxley section 302, 404, and 409 compliance.

What You Need and What You Can Expect . . . !

Process Narrations

Clearly and completely documented processes that meet the "Project Control and Reporting" requirements of the Sarbanes–Oxley Act (US).

Visual Workflows

Visual workflows for all processes, including SDLC and Change Management

Verifiable and Auditable Evidence of Outputs

Process step guidance and management approved outputs

Project process owner and management oversight for validation and continuous improvement

Document Control for Signatory Outputs

Policy for management approval and signature pages

Additional Areas of Benefit

Improved project performance, consistency, and repeatability

Continuous improvement and organizational maturity

Knowledge sharing and skills transfer among project participants

Easy integration with existing IT infrastructure, applications, and user tools

Though the majority of the Sarbanes–Oxley Act of 2002 is associated with public accounting, auditing, internal controls, and financial reporting, sections 302, 404, and 409 are written specifically to address project management and Information Technology related project and process activities. Processes On Demand helps your organization address the essential project management actions that need to be taken to ensure compliance down to the project level.

Compliance Requirement	Support of Compliance
Process: Implement a standard project management process to establish control processes and activities associated with scope, cost, and schedule.	Processes On Demand comes with a ready-to-use, proven project management process aligned to de facto standard approaches such as PMBOK® and SDLC. Processes On Demand provides a Process Builder for tailoring of additional and organization unique processes and reporting requirements.
Classification: Establish a project category or classification scheme that includes all projects associated or impacted with Sarbanes–Oxley compliance.	Processes On Demand provides project classification schemes. Projects associated with or impacted by Sarbanes–Oxley can be tracked and managed.
Documentation: Thoroughly document any changes that are made to financial systems as a result of associated IT or financial based projects.	Processes On Demand provides templates and checklists for tracking and managing changes.
Process Integration: For projects affecting any financial related system, ensure that good product and project development processes are followed.	Processes On Demand provides project and product development processes. Project management processes are integrated with product development life cycles such as product Go-to-Market (GTM) and software development life cycle (SDLC) and incorporated into the Processes On Demand.
Decision Criteria: Establish a standard stage-gate approach for all projects.	Processes On Demand provides process gates and stages, as well as reporting requirements and presentation templates. In addition, project scorecard criteria and criteria for a "go/no go" decision on projects are provided.
Risk Management: Define a risk management process that can be used to identify risks early, and to plan mitigation strategies.	Processes On Demand provides risk management and quality management processes. Workflows, process descriptions, templates, forms, and checklists are provided to identify risks and plan mitigation strategies.

It is apparent that management will have to decide how far to drill down through their processes to apply the system. The obvious criteria is, "Does this process materially affect the financial well-being of the company?" The process is all about control, risk, and monitoring. Too tight a system may be restrictive and limit innovation and creativity as well as cause resentment and frustration among employees. Too loose a system may miss important and significant activities or allow important factors to pass without remedy or attention. How far to go is a management decision and one that may have to be defended with the SEC inspectors.

Here is an overview of the Process On demand "project management" approach to compliance.

The Project Management Process

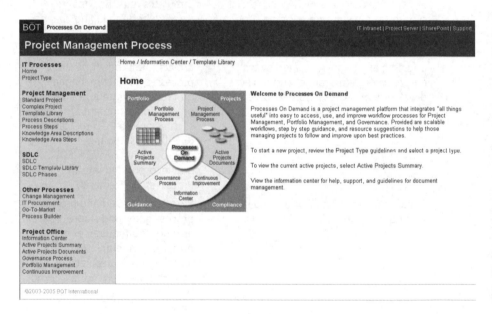

As you can see, this software covers quite a wide range of project management functions, including the specialized SDLC (Software Development Life Cycle) projects. For our purposes here, we will just look at the normal project management process to get an idea of how it fits into the Sarbanes–Oxley solution parameters. Under the Project Management heading, there are two sub-headings, one for Standard Projects, the other for Complex Projects. The Standard Project option is simply a less detailed version of the Complex Project option.

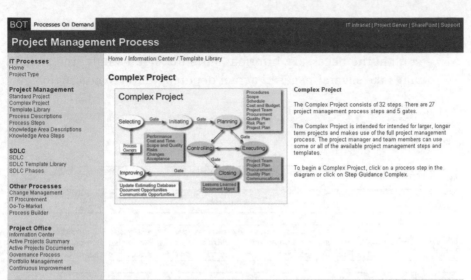

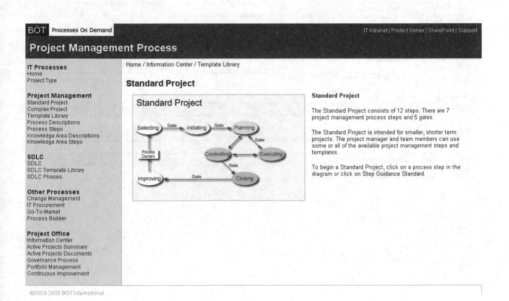

For SOX purposes, a "Project" can be a "Process" such as "debt collection", or "bill payment", it can be an "Activity" such as "bolting the wheels on" or "stacking the shelves", or it can be an actual "Project" like "develop a new product" or "open an office in Kabul." In each case the same process is followed, but to a greater or lesser extent as the "Project" warrants. Obviously some events are of more significance than others, so common sense will dictate how far to go with this process.

In each case the first step will be to define the "Project". This is done by completing the Project Proposal. The templates shown contain the necessary information fields, but a single line or field may take several pages of actual documentation to complete.

Project Management Office – We Partner to Deliver Quality Solutions

BOT

Project Proposal

Project Name:	Project Number:	Prepared by:	Date:
Customer:	Business Unit:	Contact Name:	Project Type:
			{Pick One}

INTRODUCTION Press F1 for Field Help.	*The Project Proposal provides comprehensive and convincing information supporting the work opportunity to be approved for Project Initiation. The Project Proposal should refer to the Work Request, Requirements Overview, and Business Case documents.*

Project Proposal Overview	
Sponsor	
Beneficiaries	
Business Goal	
Key Requirements	
Project Objectives	
Key Dates and Milestones	
Business Case Summary Statement	
Initial Schedule Estimates	
Initial Risks Assessments	
Summary and Recommendations	

Attachments:

☐ Work Request
☐ Requirements Overview
☐ Business case

☐ Approved for project executing.	
☐ Not approved for project executing.	
Approving Authority	**Signature and Date**

Throughout this process, there are three categories to be maintained.

Operations: The meat and potatoes of the project, what it is, how it is to be accomplished, who is involved, benefits, risks, and logistics.

Financial Reporting: Tracking, control, and analysis of the financial aspects of the project, probably including the auditing and monitoring functions. Final reports and accounting.

Compliance: Ensuring compliance to existing laws, regulations, rules, and permits.

The Information Technology (IT) department provides the overall information processing system to obtain, record, process, analyze, and report the entire process.

Once the Project Proposal is completed and agreed upon, the Project Charter is created to authenticate and initiate the Project.

Project Charter

Project Name:	Project Number:	Prepared by:	Date:
Customer:	**Business Unit:**	**Contact Name:**	**Project Type:**
			{Pick One}

INTRODUCTION Press F1 for Field Help.	*The Project Charter describes the project in further detail and is the document of record to be used as input into the project plan. The project charter should use and reference information from the Work Request, Requirements Overview, Project Proposal, and Business Case.*

PROJECT CONTROL INFORMATION

Project Manager			Project Sponsor	
Business Units Involved	Core Team Members	Responsibility and Authority	Responsible Manager	Signature and Date

PROJECT CHARTER SCOPE

Beneficiaries	
Business Goal	
Key Requirements	
Project Objectives	
Deliverables	
Business Case Summary Statement	

SCHEDULE

BUDGET

RESOURCES OTHER THAN CORE TEAM MEMBERS

RISKS ASSESSMENTS

SUMMARY AND RECOMMENDATIONS

Attachments:

Project Proposal
Business Case

The Risk Response template shows how identified risks are to be handled.

Project Management Office – We Partner to Deliver Quality Solutions

BOT

Risk Response Plan and Register

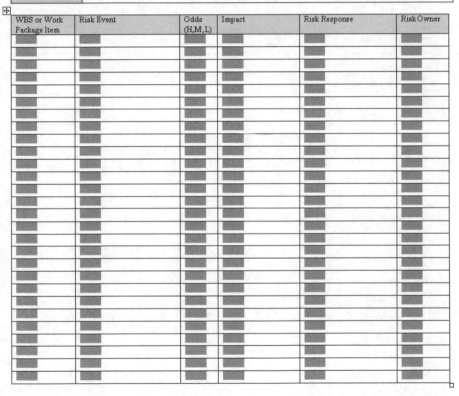

Project Name:	Project Number:	Prepared by:	Date:
Customer:	Business Unit:	Contact Name:	Project Type:
			{Pick One}

INTRODUCTION Press F1 for Field Help.	*The Risk Response Plan and Register shows the risk response and register information for each component of the work breakdown structure.*

WBS or Work Package Item	Risk Event	Odds (H,M,L)	Impact	Risk Response	Risk Owner

The Business Case template ensures that the financial implications of the project are clearly defined and described.

Business Case Template

Project Name:	Project Number:	Prepared by:	Date:
Customer:	Business Unit:	Contact Name:	Project Type:
			{Pick One}

INTRODUCTION Press F1 for Field Help.	*The Business Case is a document that states the costs and benefits for a proposed project. Non-financial benefits and identifiable risks are also stated.*

Business Case Summary

Project Alignment with Strategic Priorities		
Benefits Summary Statement		
Time Period of Benefits Realized		
Total Benefits Estimated		
Total Funding Requested		
Financial Measurements	Breakeven Point	
	Net Present Value (NPV)	
	Return on Investment	

Financial Summary

Measurements	One-Time	Year 1	Year 2	Year 3	Year 4	Year 5
Increased Revenue						
Decreased Expenses						
Total Benefits						
Total Costs						

Non-Financial Summary

Intangible Benefits	
Intangible Costs	

Risk Assessment

Cost	

COST DETAILS

Costs Details

Costs	Item	Year 1	Year 2	Year 3	Year 4	Year 5	Total
Direct Items							
Indirect Items							
Total Costs							
Expense							
Expense Items							
Apportioned Overheads							
General and Administrative							
Time and Materials							
Totals							

The BOT Software provides a comprehensive list of templates that cover pretty well every aspect of project management, and they can be modified to suit specific requirements of SOX compliance such as internal auditing and monitoring reports. Here is the list.

Project Management Process

IT Processes
Home
Project Type

Project Management
Standard Project
Complex Project
Template Library
Process Descriptions
Process Steps
Knowledge Area Descriptions
Knowledge Area Steps

SDLC
SDLC
SDLC Template Library
SDLC Phases

Other Processes
Change Management
IT Procurement
Go-To-Market
Process Builder

Project Office
Information Center
Active Projects Summary
Active Projects Documents
Governance Process
Portfolio Management
Continuous Improvement

Template Library

Standard Project	Complex Project
Project Selection	**Project Selection**
1.0 Project Selection	1.0 Project Selection
Work Request	Work Request
Requirements Overview	Requirements Overview
Project Proposal	Project Proposal
Business Case	Business Case
Project Determination Checklist	Project Determination Checklist
Project Type Checklist	Project Type Checklist
Project Selection Scorecard	Project Selection Scorecard
Project Selection Scorecard Spreadsheet	Project Selection Scorecard Spreadsheet
Project Selection Checklist	Project Selection Checklist
1.99 Project Selection Gate	1.99 Project Selection Gate
Project Selection Approval	Project Selection Approval
Project Selection Meeting Agenda	Project Selection Meeting Agenda
Initiating	**Initiating**
2.0 Initiating	2.0 Initiating
Project Charter	Project Charter
Initiating Process Checklist	Initiating Process Checklist
2.99 Initiating Gate	2.99 Initiating Gate
Charter Approval Document	Charter Approval Document
Project Charter Meeting Agenda	Project Charter Meeting Agenda
Planning	**Planning**
3.0 Planning	3.1 Procedures
Requirements Document	Project Procedures Document
Work Breakdown Structure	3.2 Scope
Project Schedule	Requirements Document
Project Schedule (Excel)	Scope Statement
Project Schedule (MS Project)	Work Breakdown Structure
Work Package	Work Package
Work Package List	Work Package List
Project Budget	Work Breakdown Structure Checklist
Project Plan	3.3 Schedule
Project Plan Checklist	Project Schedule
Planning Process Checklist	Project Schedule (Excel)
3.99 Planning Gate	Project Schedule (MS Project)
Project Plan Approval Document	Work Package
Project Plan Approval Meeting Agenda	Project Schedule Checklist
Executing	3.4 Cost and Budget
4.0 Executing	Cost Estimates Document
Kick Off Meeting Checklist	Project Budget
Kick Off Meeting Agenda	Work Package
Project Team Organization Chart	Project Budget Checklist
The Product of the Project	3.5 Project Team
Project Status Report	Project Organization Chart
Quality Report	Project Organization Chart (PowerPoint)
Project Issues Log	Team Directory
Change Request Form	Responsibility Assignment Matrix
Change Request Log	Key Team Sign Offs
Controlling	Work Package
5.0 Controlling	3.6 Procurement Plan
Project Performance Report	Procurement Plan
Project Transition Report	Procurement Statement of Work
Controlling Process Checklist	Procurement Contract Selection Report
Issues/Changes Requests Log Meeting Agenda	Procurement Contract Selection Spreadsheet
Project Status Report Meeting Agenda	Procurement Planning Checklist
Project Plan Changes Meeting Agenda	3.7 Quality Plan
5.99 Controlling Gate	Quality Plan
Product Acceptance Document	Work Package
Closing	3.8 Risk Plan
6.0 Closing	Risk Response Plan and Register
Lessons Learned Document	Work Package
Project Archives Report	3.9 Project Plan
Closing Process Checklist	Project Plan
6.99 Closing Gate	Work Package
Closing Approval Document	Project Plan Checklist
Project Closing Meeting Agenda	Planning Process Checklist
Continuous Improvement	3.99 Planning Gate
7.0 Continuous Improvement	Project Plan Approval Document
Continuous Improvement Document	Project Plan Approval Meeting Agenda
Communications Checklist	**Executing**
Continuous Improvement Meeting Agenda	4.1 Project Team
	Kick Off Meeting Checklist
	Kick Off Meeting Agenda
	Project Team Organization Chart
	Individual Performance Assessment
	Project Manager Performance
	Team Performance
	4.2 Project Plan
	The Product of the Project
	Project Issues Log
	Change Request Form
	Change Request Log
	4.3 Procurement Plan
	Specifications
	Request For Proposal
	Procurement Contracts Report
	Contract Formation Checklist
	4.4 Quality Plan
	Quality Report
	4.5 Communications
	Project Status Report
	Controlling
	5.1 Performance
	Project Performance Report
	5.2 Cost and Time
	Budget Update Proposal
	Schedule Change Proposal
	5.3 Scope and Quality
	Quality/Scope Change Proposal
	5.4 Risks
	Risk Register Change Proposal
	5.5 Changes
	Approved Changes
	Project Plan Changes Log
	Issues/Changes Requests Log Meeting Agenda
	Project Status Report Meeting Agenda
	Project Plan Changes Meeting Agenda
	5.99 Controlling Gate
	Product Acceptance Document
	Closing
	6.1 Lessons Learned
	Lessons Learned Document
	Project Performance Feedback
	6.2 Document Management
	Project Archives Report
	Closing Process Checklist
	6.3 Closing Gate
	Closing Approval Document
	Project Closing Meeting Agenda
	Continuous Improvement
	7.1 Update Estimating Database
	Estimating Databases Update
	7.2 Document Process Improvements
	Continuous Improvement Document
	7.3 Communicate Process Improvements
	Communications Checklist
	Continuous Improvement Meeting Agenda

The Sarbanes-Oxley Act

183

Once the Charter is accepted, the Project Team can develop the Project Plan. This document will range from being one or two pages for simple activities or processes, to significant volumes for large projects. For example it may contain a detailed requirements analysis.

Project Management Office – We Partner to Deliver Quality Solutions   BOT

Requirements Document

Project Name:	Project Number:	Prepared by:	Date:
Customer:	Business Unit:	Contact Name:	Project Type:
			{Pick One}

INTRODUCTION Press F1 for Field Help.	*The Requirements Document consists of a number of inputs that help describe the requirements and specifications of the product of the project.*

Control Information	
Project Name	
Project Objectives	
Product Name	
Product Purpose	
Approach to Requirements	
Analysis of Stakeholder Needs	
Source of Requirements	
Validation of Requirements	
Impact Analysis	
Product Requirements	
Features	
Functions	
Measurable User Benefits	
Other Requirements	

Attachments:

- Business Case
- Engineering Drawings
- Index of Terminology
- Other

Once the Project Plan is completed, the project can get under way.

Project Plan

Project Name:	Project Number:	Prepared by:	Date:
Customer:	Business Unit:	Contact Name:	Project Type:
			{Pick One}

INTRODUCTION Press F1 for Field Help.	*The Project Plan is the outline for the project. The project plan refers to other documents as needed.*

Project Plan	Management Summary
Goals	
Objectives	
Scope	
Schedule	
Budget	
Resources	
Risks	
Summary	

Attachments:

- ☐ Project Charter
- ☐ Project Budget
- ☐ Project Schedule
- ☐ Requirements Document
- ☐ Scope Statement
- ☐ Work Breakdown Structure
- ☐ Work Package List
- ☐ Work Packages
- ☐ Project Team Organization Chart
- ☐ Procurement Plan
- ☐ Quality Plan
- ☐ Risk Plan
- ☐ Other

As the project proceeds, it is subject to ongoing scrutiny to ensure that progress is satisfactory, budgets are not being significantly exceeded, change requests are being dealt with, and risks are constantly being anticipated and controlled. The Project Manager will produce periodic reports indicating how the project is progressing.

Project Management Office – We Partner to Deliver Quality Solutions

BOT

Project Status Report

Project Name:	Project Number:	Prepared by:	Date:
Customer:	Business Unit:	Contact Name:	Project Type:
			{Pick One}

INTRODUCTION Press F1 for Field Help.	*The Project Status Report is a summary of the project status. For each work activity of the project, the planned and actual performances are shown.*

Project Status Report						Report Date	

Project Status	Status Report Summary						
☐ Project in jeopardy							
☐ Project late and/or over budget							
☐ Project on time on budget							

Project Activity	Start		Finish		Effort	
	Planned	Actual	Planned	Actual	Planned	Actual

Project Variance Types	Description of Variances
☐ Scope Change ☐ Resources not Available ☐ Estimating Error ☐ Performance Error ☐ Other	

Working with the Project Manager, the Internal Auditor will report regularly on the status of the project with particular emphasis on the financial aspects, risk identification and amelioration, and completion prospects.

Project Performance Report

Project Name:	Project Number:	Prepared by:	Date:
Customer:	Business Unit:	Contact Name:	Project Type: [Pick One]

INTRODUCTION Press F1 for Field Help	The Project Performance Report shows the performance of the project. The task manager completes task performance information and the project manager completes the project performance report.

Project Performance Report

WBS Task	Task Performance			Cost/Schedule Data			Cost Performance			Schedule Performance		
	Percent Complete	Weeks to Complete	Expense $/Week	Planned Value (PV)	Earned Value (EV)	Actual Cost (AC)	Cost Variance (CV)	Cost Variance Percentage (CVP)	Cost Performance Index (CPI)	Schedule Variance ($) (SV)	Schedule Variance % (SVP)	Schedule Performance Index (SPI)
Totals												

Analysis and Comments

Estimate at Completion (EAC)		Manager	Department	Signature	Date
Budget at Completion (BAC)		Task Manager			
Variance at Completion (VAC)		Project Manager			

Upon completion of the project, the Closing Process checklist is filled in.

Project Management Office – We Partner to Deliver Quality Solutions

BOT

Closing Process Checklist

Project Name:	Project Number:	Prepared by:	Date:
Customer:	**Business Unit:**	**Contact Name:**	**Project Type:**
			[Pick One]

INTRODUCTION Press F1 for Field Help.	*The Closing Process Checklist provides assessment guidelines to review upon completion of the project to help ensure that the closing process is followed and is effective.*

Tick	Closing Process Checklist
☐	All work packages are completed.
☐	All deliverables are accepted.
☐	All project commitments are met.
☐	All project costs are correctly charged to the project.
☐	Unfinished work packages have been documented and explained.
☐	Remaining work has been negotiated with the project sponsor.
☐	Resources are dedicated and committed to finishing remaining work.
☐	Management has been notified of project closing.
☐	The project plan and supporting data has been archived.
☐	Other

Every project has strengths and weaknesses, problems and solutions that can be learned from. The participants in the project are invited to submit their own comments based on their individual participation in the project.

Lessons Learned Document

Project Name:	Project Number:	Prepared by:	Date:
Customer:	Business Unit:	Contact Name:	Project Type:
			{Pick One}

INTRODUCTION Press F1 for Field Help.	*The Lessons Learned Document is the document of record for improvement feedback in the project management process. Lessons learned may address any area of possible improvement.*

Lessons Learned Document			
Summary	Project Background		
	Summary of Lessons Learned		
	Overall Recommendations		
Process Performance	Project Selection	Observations	
		Improvements	
	Initiating	Observations	
		Improvements	
	Planning	Observations	
		Improvements	
	Executing	Observations	
		Improvements	
	Controlling	Observations	
		Improvements	
	Closing	Observations	
		Improvements	
Tools Performance	Observations		
	Improvements		
Team Performance	Observations		
	Team Improvements		
Schedule Performance	Observations		
	Schedule Improvements		
Cost Performance	Observations		
	Cost Improvements		
Quality Performance	Observations		
	Quality Improvements		
Other Areas		Observations	
		Improvements	

Project Manager(s) and Auditors and, depending on the size of the project, Department Heads and Team Leaders can complete a "Continuous Improvement" document based on the findings of the "Lessons Learned" document as well as their own personal experience with the project. Too frequently time and money are wasted re-inventing the wheel in subsequent projects, and carefully and completely winding up a project by attending to these details can save money, time, and mistakes next time around.

Project Management Office – We Partner to Deliver Quality Solutions

BOT

Continuous Improvement Document

Project Name:	Project Number:	Prepared by:	Date:
Customer:	Business Unit:	Contact Name:	Project Type:
			{Pick One}

INTRODUCTION Press F1 for Field Help.	*The Continuous Improvements Document is intended provide documented improvement opportunities based upon project experiences and observations.*

RECOMMENDED CONTINUOUS IMPROVEMENT

Recommended Continuous Improvements		
Process Area	Description of Problem	Recommendations for Improvement
Project Selection		
Initiating		
Planning		
Executing		
Controlling		
Closing		
Continuous Improvement		
Portfolio Management Processes		
Inventory		
Evaluate		
Prioritize		
Balance		
Review		
Other		
Tools		
Training		
Other		

Project team participants, management, and auditors can review the status of the project portfolio and evidence of compliance to the control process. An executive dashboard is provided to summarize the project status for top projects and SOX projects. Additionally, users can access further project information as they seamlessly navigate from Processes On Demand to supporting platforms such as

Microsoft SharePoint, etc., for document management, and Microsoft Project Server, etc., for resource management.

Looking at the image of the Summary you can see how each element, whether it is a Project, a Process, or an Activity can be tracked on a continuing basis with any problem areas showing up clearly. Needless to say, the effectiveness of this, or any system, relies heavily on the reliability, honesty, and consistency of the individuals who are reporting and the supervisors who are evaluating and tracking the information as it comes available.

Given that these conditions prevail, management can be confident that they are as well informed concerning the ongoing health and progress of their company as they can expect to be, and can sign-off their reports with confidence, and with the knowledge that they really do know what is going on in their company.

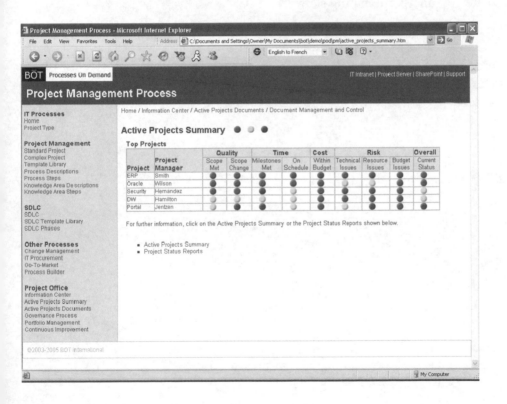

Summary

This has been a very simplified view of the project management approach to SOX compliance. It may not be the appropriate methodology for every company, and it does rely on a company having an adequate financial control system already in place which can be integrated with the Project Management system to cover the spectrum of SOX compliance.

The CFO and his accounting department, together with the CIO and the information technology specialists, will probably be the people responsible for structuring the entire, comprehensive system which will ensure not only that the company is in compliance so the CFO and CEO stay out of jail and remain solvent, but that the company can benefit from the introduction of the control systems through improved efficiency, better communications, and a more informed and participating staff.

Index

Index

197